Middle Grades

ASSESSMENT PACKAGE

2

BERKELEY
HARVARD
MICHIGAN STATE
SHELL CENTRE

Balanced Assessment for the
Mathematics Curriculum

UNIVERSITY of NORTHERN
BRITISH COLUMBIA
LIBRARY
Prince George, B.C.
DISCARD

Dale Seymour Publications®

Project Directors: Hugh Burkhardt
Phil Daro
Jim Ridgway
Judah Schwartz
Sandra Wilcox

Managing Editor: Catherine Anderson

Acquisitions Editor: Merle Silverman

Project Editor: Toni-Ann Guadagnoli

Production/Manufacturing Director: Janet Yearian

Senior Production/Manufacturing Coordinator: Fiona Santoianni

Design Director: Phyllis Aycock

Design Manager: Jeff Kelly

Cover and Interior Design: Don Taka

Cover Image: Hutchings Photography

Illustrator: Larry Nolte

Composition: Joe Conte

The work of this project was supported by a grant from the National Science Foundation.
The opinions expressed in these materials do not necessarily represent the position, policy,
or endorsement of the Foundation.

Copyright © 2000 by the Regents of the University of California. All rights reserved.

This book is published by Dale Seymour Publications®,
an imprint of Addison Wesley Longman, Inc.

Dale Seymour Publications
10 Bank Street
White Plains, NY 10602-5026
Customer Service: 800-872-1100

Limited reproduction permission: The publisher grants permission to individual teachers who have
purchased this book to reproduce the blackline masters as needed for use with their own students.
Reproduction for an entire school or school district or for commercial use is prohibited.

Printed in the United States of America
Order number 33004
ISBN 0-7690-0067-3

1-2-3-4-5-6-7-ML-02-01-00-99

This product is printed
on recycled paper

Authors

This assessment package was designed and developed by members of the Balanced Assessment Project team, particularly Judith Zawojewski, Mary Bouck, John Gillespie, Sandra Wilcox, Helene Alpert, Angela Krebs, Faaiz Gierdien, Whitney Johnson, and Kyle Ward. The editor was Mary Bouck.

Many others have made helpful comments and suggestions in the course of the development. We thank them all. The project is particularly grateful to the mathematics consultants, teachers, and students with whom these tasks were developed and tested, particularly Josh Coty, Ray Fauch, Julie Faulkner, Loraine Gawlik, Yvonne Grant, Lisa Harden, Liz Jones, Terri Keusch, Tom Little, Tammy McCarthy, Jan Palkowski, Marlene Robinson, Mark Rudd, Nancy Rudd, Mary Beth Schmitt, Janet Small, Judy Vandermeulen, Patti Wagner, and Mike Wilson.

The project was directed by Alan Schoenfeld, Hugh Burkhardt, Phil Daro, Jim Ridgway, Judah Schwartz, and Sandra Wilcox.

The package consists of materials compiled or adapted from work done at the four sites of the Balanced Assessment Project:

Balanced Assessment
Graduate School of Education
University of California
Berkeley, CA 94720-1670
USA

Balanced Assessment (MARS)
513 Erickson Hall
Michigan State University
East Lansing, MI 48824
USA

Balanced Assessment
Educational Technology Center
Harvard University
Cambridge, MA 02138
USA

Balanced Assessment
Shell Centre for Mathematical Education
University of Nottingham
Nottingham NG7 2RD
England

Additional tasks and packages, the materials in their original form, and other assessment resources such as guides to scoring may be obtained from the project sites. For a full list of available publications, and for further information, contact the Project's Mathematics Assessment Resource Service (MARS) at the Michigan State address above. We welcome your comments.

Table of Contents

What is balanced assessment?

Mathematics assessments tell us and our students how well they are learning mathematics. A carefully designed mathematics assessment should:

■ assess the mathematics that counts, focusing on important ideas and processes;

■ be fair to the students, providing them with a set of opportunities to demonstrate what they know and can do;

■ be fair to the curriculum, offering a balance of opportunities—long and short tasks, basic knowledge and problem solving, individual and group work, and the spectrum of concepts and processes that reflect the vision of the NCTM *Standards;*

■ be of such high quality that students and teachers learn from them—so that assessment time serves as instructional time, and assessment and curriculum live in harmony;

■ provide useful information to administrators, so they can judge the effectiveness of their programs; to teachers, so they can judge the quality of their instruction; and to students and parents, so they can see where the students are doing well and where more work is needed.

This is such an assessment package, dealing with the mathematics appropriate for the middle grades. It was designed by the Balanced Assessment Project, an NSF-supported collaboration that was funded to create a series of exemplary assessment items and packages for assessing students' mathematical performance at various grade levels (elementary grades, middle grades, high school, and advanced high school). Balanced Assessment offers a wide range of extensively field-tested tasks and packages—some paper-and-pencil, some high-tech or multimedia—and consulting services to help states and districts implement meaningful and informative mathematics assessments.

What is balance?

It's easy to see what isn't balanced. An assessment that focuses on computation only is out of balance. So is one that focuses on patterns, functions, and algebra to the exclusion of geometry, shape, and space, or that ignores or gives a cursory nod toward statistics and probability. Likewise, assessments that do not provide students with ample opportunity to show how they can reason or communicate mathematically are unbalanced. These are content and process dimensions of balance, but there are many others—length of task, whether tasks are pure or applied, and so on. The following table shows some of the dimensions used to design and balance this package.
(For explanations of terms that may be unfamiliar, see the Glossary.)

Dimensions of Balance

Mathematical Content Dimension

- **Mathematical content** will include some of the following:

  Number and Quantity including: concepts and representation; computation; estimation and measurement; number theory and general number properties.

  Patterns, Functions, and Algebra including: patterns and generalization; functional relationships (including ratio and proportion); graphical and tabular representation; symbolic representation; forming and solving relationships.

  Geometry, Shape, and Space including: shape, properties of shapes, relationships; spatial representation, visualization, and construction; location and movement; transformation and symmetry; trigonometry.

  Handling Data, Statistics, and Probability including: collecting, representing, and interpreting data; probability models—experimental and theoretical; simulation.

  Other Mathematics including: discrete mathematics, including combinatorics; underpinnings of calculus; mathematical structures.

Mathematical Process Dimension

- **Phases** of problem solving, reasoning, and communication will include, as broad categories, some or all of the following: modeling and formulating; transforming and manipulating; inferring and drawing conclusions; checking and evaluating; reporting.

Task Type Dimensions

- **Task Type** will be one of the following: open investigation; nonroutine problem; design; plan; evaluation and recommendation; review and critique; re-presentation of information; technical exercise; definition of concepts.

- **Nonroutineness** in: context; mathematical aspects or results; mathematical connections.

- **Openness:** It may have an open end with open questions; open middle.

- **Type of Goal** is one of the following: pure mathematics; illustrative application of the mathematics; applied power over the practical situation.

- **Reasoning Length** is the expected time for the longest section of the task. (It is an indication of the amount of "scaffolding"—the detailed step-by-step guidance that the prompt may provide.)

Circumstances of Performance Dimensions

- **Task Length:** ranging from short tasks (10–20 minutes), through long tasks (30–45 minutes), to extended tasks (several days to several weeks).

- **Modes of Presentation:** written; oral; video; computer.

- **Modes of Working** on the task: individual; group; mixed.

- **Modes of Response** by the student: written; built; spoken; programmed; performed.

What's in a package?

A typical Balanced Assessment Package offers ten to twenty tasks, ranging in length from 5 to 45 minutes. Some of the tasks consist of a single problem, while others consist of a sequence of problems. Taken together, the tasks provide students with an opportunity to display their knowledge and skills across the broad spectrum of content and processes described in the NCTM *Standards*. It takes time to get this kind of rich information—but the problems are mathematically rich and well worth the time spent on them.

What's included with each task?

We have tried to provide you with as much information as possible about the mathematics central to solving a task, about managing the assessment, and about typical student responses and how to analyze the mathematics in them. Each section of this package, corresponding to one task, consists of the following:

Overview   The first page of each section provides a quick overview that lets you see whether the task is appropriate for use at any particular point in the curriculum. This overview includes the following:

- Task Description—the situation that students will be asked to investigate or solve.

- Assumed Mathematical Background—the kinds of previous experiences students will need to have had to engage the task productively.

- Core Elements of Performance—the mathematical ideas and processes that will be central to the task.

- Circumstances—the estimated time for students to work on the task; the special materials that the task will require; whether students will work individually, in pairs, or in small groups; and any other such information.

Task Prompt   These papers are intended for the student. To make them easy to find, they have been designed with stars in the margin and a white bar across the top. The task prompt begins with a statement for the student characterizing the aims of the task. In some cases there is a pre-assessment activity that teachers assign in advance of the formal assessment. In some cases there is a launch activity that familiarizes students with the context but is not part of the formal assessment.

Sample Solution   Each task is accompanied by at least one solution; where there are multiple approaches to a problem, more than one may appear.

Using this Task   Here we provide suggestions about launching the task and helping students understand the context of the problem. Some tasks have pre-activities; some have students do some initial exploration in pairs or as a whole class to become familiar with the context while the formal assessment is done individually. Information from field-testing about challenging aspects of tasks is given here. We may also include suggestions for subsequent instruction related to the task, as well as extensions that can be used for assessment or instructional purposes.

Characterizing Performance   This section contains descriptions of characteristic student responses that the task is likely to elicit. These descriptions, based on the *Core Elements of Performance*, indicate various levels of successful engagement with the task. They are accompanied by annotated artists' renderings of typical student work. These illustrations will prepare you to assess the wide range of responses produced by your students. We have chosen examples that show something of the range and variety of responses to the task, and the various aspects of mathematical performance it calls for. The commentary is intended to exemplify these key aspects of performance at various levels across several domains. Teachers and others have found both the examples and the commentary extremely useful; its purpose is to bring out explicitly for each task the wide range of mathematical performance that the standards imply.

Scoring student work

The discussions of student work in the section *Characterizing Performance* are deliberately qualitative and holistic, avoiding too much detail. They are designed to focus on the mathematical ideas that "count," summarized in the *Core Elements of Performance* for each task. They offer a guide to help teachers and students look in some depth at a student's work in the course of instruction, considering how it might be improved.

For some other purposes, we need more. Formal assessment, particularly if the results are used for life-critical decisions, demands more accurate scoring, applied consistently across different scorers. This needs more precise rubrics, linked to a clear scheme for reporting on performance. These can be in a variety of styles, each of which has different strengths. The Balanced Assessment Project has developed resources that support a range of styles.

For example, *holistic approaches* require the scorer to take a balanced overall view of the student's response, relating general criteria of quality in performance to the specific item. *Point scoring approaches* draw attention in detail to the various aspects of performance that the task involves, provide a natural mechanism for balancing greater strength in one aspect with some weakness in another, and are useful for *aggregating scores*.

How to use this package

This assessment package may be used in a variety of ways, depending on your local needs and circumstances.

- You may want to implement formal performance assessment under controlled conditions at the school, district, or state level. This package provides a balanced set of tasks appropriate for such on-demand, high-stakes assessment.

- You may want to provide opportunities for classroom-based performance assessment, embedded within the curriculum, under less-controlled conditions. This package allows you the discretion of selecting tasks that are appropriate for use at particular points in the curriculum.

- You may be looking for tasks to serve as a transition toward a curriculum as envisioned in the NCTM *Standards* or as enrichment for existing curriculum. In this case, the tasks in this package can serve as rich instructional problems to enhance your curriculum. They are exemplars of the kinds of instructional tasks that will support performance assessment and can be used for preparing students for future performance assessment. Even in these situations, the tasks provide you with rich sites to engage in informal assessment of student understanding.

Preparing for the assessment

We urge you to work through a task yourself before giving it to your students. This gives you an opportunity to become familiar with the context and the mathematical demands of the task, and to anticipate what might need to be highlighted in launching the task.

It is important to have at hand all the necessary materials students need to engage a task before launching them on the task. We assume that students have certain tools and materials available at all times in the mathematics classroom and that these will be accessible to students to choose from during any assessment activity.

At the middle grades these resources include: grid paper and square and isometric dot paper; dice, square tiles, cubes, and other concrete materials; calculators; rulers, compasses, and protractors or angle rulers; scissors, markers, tape, string, paper clips, and glue.

If a task requires any special materials, these are specified in the task.

Managing the assessment

We anticipate that this package will be used in a variety of situations. Therefore, our guidance about managing assessment is couched in fairly general suggestions. We point out some considerations you may want to take into account under various circumstances.

The way in which any particular task is introduced to students will vary. The launch will be shaped by a number of considerations (for example, the students, the complexity of the instructions, the degree of familiarity students have with the context of the problem). In some cases it will be necessary only to distribute the task to students and then let them read and work through the task. Other situations may call for you to read the task to the class to assure that everyone understands the instructions, the context, and the aim of the assessment. Decisions of this kind will be influenced by the ages of the students, their experiences with reading mathematical tasks, their fluency in English, and any difficulties in reading that might exclude them from otherwise productively engaging with the mathematics of the task.

Under conditions of formal assessment, once students have been set to work on a task, the teacher should not intervene except where specified. This is essential in formal, high-stakes assessment but it is important under any assessment circumstance. Even the slightest intervention—reinterpreting instructions, suggesting ways to begin, offering prompts when students appear to be stuck—has the potential to alter the task for the student significantly. However, you should provide general encouragement within a supportive classroom environment as a normal part of doing mathematics in school. This includes reminding students about the aim of the assessment (using the words at the beginning of the task prompt), when the period of assessment is nearing an end, and how to turn in their work when they have completed the task.

We suggest a far more relaxed use of the package when students are meeting these kinds of tasks for the first time, particularly in situations where they are being used primarily as learning tasks to enhance the curriculum. Under these circumstances you may reasonably decide to do some coaching, talk with students as they work on a task, pose questions when they seem to get stuck. In these instances you may be using the tasks for informal assessment—observing what strategies students favor, what kinds of questions they ask, what they seem to understand and what they are struggling with, what kinds of prompts get them unstuck. This can be extremely useful information in helping you make ongoing instructional and assessment decisions. However, as students have more experiences with these kinds of tasks, the amount of coaching you do should decline and students should rely less on this kind of assistance.

Under conditions of formal assessment, you will need to make decisions about how tasks will be scored and by whom, how scores will be aggregated across tasks, and how students' accomplishments will be reported to interested constituencies. These decisions will, of necessity, be made at the school, district, or state level and will likely reflect educational, political, and economic considerations specific to the local context.

Long Tasks	Task Type	Circumstances of Performance
1. Toothpicks	45-minute problem; pure mathematics; nonroutine mathematical connections; open-ended	individual assessment
2. Camp Placement	45-minute evaluation and recommendation; applied power in student life; nonroutine mathematical connections; open-ended	pair assessment
3. Matting a Photo	45-minute design; applied power in adult life; nonroutine context	individual assessment after entry work in pairs
4. Grocery Store	45-minute problem; applied power; nonroutine context from adult life	individual assessment after entry work in pairs
5. Pentagon	40-minute problem with several short tasks; pure mathematics; nonroutine mathematical connections	individual assessment
6. Lucky Draw	40-minute evaluation and recommendation task; applied power in nonroutine context from student life	individual assessment after a whole-class introduction
7. Brian's T-shirt	30-minute re-presentation task; nonroutine student-life context; open middle	individual assessment

* For explanations of terms that may be unfamiliar, see the Glossary, and the *Dimensions of Balance* table in the Introduction.

Mathematical Content	Mathematical Processes
Patterns, functions, and algebra: patterns; forming functional relationships; tabular and symbolic representation; properties of shapes	formulation of relationships through generalizing patterns; simplifying them by manipulation
Data and statistics: analysis of given data; rank ordering; grouping; evaluation over several variables	balance of interpretation and evaluation of the data; formulation of a model for grouping; evaluation and justification; communication of reasons
Geometry, space, and shape: location and symmetry, using properties of rectangles	some formulation of the approach and mainly of the consequent instructions; manipulation to work out the detail; communication
Patterns, functions, and algebra with number: measurement; generalizing; forming and solving relationships; symbolic representation	manipulation of the measurement, formulation of the relationship; communication of the results and the reasoning behind them
Geometry, space, and shape: locate points and determine slopes; angular properties of shapes; trigonometry; perpendicular and parallel lines	manipulation with some formulation
Data, statistics, and probability: probability concepts; combining and comparing probabilities; simulation of a game	formulation and manipulation of the probability model (theoretical or experimental); evaluation and communication of advice
Geometry, space, and shape: construct a system to locate points, lines, and circles on a grid to form a given pattern	formulation of the system; manipulation of the coordinates; communication in a clear message, with checks

Expanded Table of Contents

Mathematical Content	Mathematical Processes
Geometry, space, and shape: area properties of circles; comparisons	mainly manipulation; straightforward application of the area formula; some formulation of approach
Number and quantity: concepts of and computation with decimals	mainly manipulation and evaluation of results; clear-minded formulation needed
Geometry, space, and shape: angle properties of regular polygons, their perimeters and areas; visualization	mainly manipulation
Data, statistics, and probability: bar graph interpretation; mean and median measures	interpretation of graphical data; manipulation; evaluation of results
Patterns, functions, and algebra: generalize a pattern sequence to form a functional relationship, linear in n	interpretation and analysis of the pattern sequence; formulation of the relationship; communication to a fellow student
Number and quantity: use theory of factors and primes; compute and evaluate possibilities	formulation of a strategy; manipulation to compute factors; evaluation of the clues
Data, statistics, and probability: compose a bar graph; choose mean or median measure of center; justify	interpretation of data; manipulation in forming a graph, and computation of measures; evaluation of results
Geometry, space, and shape, with number: properties of rectangles; compute complete set of possibilities	concept-based manipulation
Geometry, space, and shape: side and angle properties of similar and congruent triangles, formed by a grid of parallel lines	mainly manipulation, with some formulation of the approach
Geometry, space, and shape, with number: properties of triangles and rectangles; symmetry; fractions	formulation of a dissection of the square; manipulation to compute the fractions
Geometry, space, and shape, with number: properties of rectangles; compute complete set of possibilities	concept-based manipulation

1

Toothpicks

Investigate and generalize patterns.

Use numerical and/or visual reasoning.

Identify functional behavior.

Long Task

Task Description

Students investigate stair-shaped figures made of toothpicks. As the figures increase in size, students determine the perimeter and total number of toothpicks needed to make additional figures. They find and explain rules for determining these values and discuss the functional behavior. Finally, students create and answer questions about their own increasing toothpick designs.

Assumed Mathematical Background

It is assumed that students have had experience with finding and describing patterns in a geometric context and with generalizing patterns symbolically.

Core Elements of Performance

- extend patterns to find values for additional figures
- use numerical and/or visual reasoning to find and symbolically describe rules
- identify functional behavior and justify choice
- create and generalize rules for their own growing toothpick design

Circumstances

Grouping:	Students complete an individual written response.
Materials:	square dot paper, toothpicks (for overhead demonstration), and graphing calculators (optional)
Estimated time:	45 minutes

Toothpicks

This problem gives you the chance to

- *investigate, extend, symbolically generalize, and create patterns*
- *use numerical and/or visual reasoning*
- *discuss functional behavior*

The figures shown below are made with toothpicks.

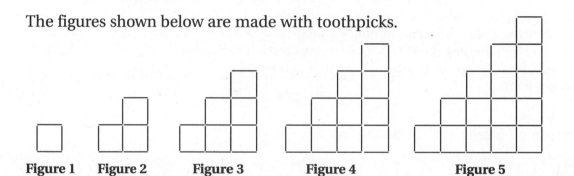

Figure 1   **Figure 2**   **Figure 3**   **Figure 4**   **Figure 5**

1. Make a table to the right showing:
   a. the number of the figure
   b. the perimeter of the figure
      (in number of toothpicks)
   c. the total number of toothpicks
      (needed to make the figure)

2. Extending the pattern, what is the perimeter of **Figure 6?**
   Show or explain how you figured this out.

3. How many toothpicks are needed to make **Figure 7?** Show or
   explain how you figured this out.

© The Regents of the University of California

4. Write a formula that could be used to find the **perimeter** of any Figure *N*. Tell what your variables represent.

5. Write a formula that could be used to find the **total number of toothpicks** needed to make any Figure *N*. Tell what your variables represent.

6. Is the growth of the **perimeter** linear, quadratic, or exponential? Give reasons for your decision.

7. Is the growth of the **total number of toothpicks** linear, quadratic, or exponential? Give reasons for your decision.

8. Create your own toothpick pattern.

   a. Show at least **5** different figures of your pattern that show how the figure changes as it grows. Make sure it is clear how to continue your pattern.

   b. Write an equation or rule that could be used to find the **perimeter** of any size of your design (Figure *N*).

   c. Write an equation or rule that could be used to find the **total number of toothpicks** needed for any size of your design (Figure *N*).

© The Regents of the University of California

Task **A Sample Solution**

1.

Figure number	Perimeter	Total number of toothpicks
1	4	4
2	8	10
3	12	18
4	16	28
5	20	40

2. The perimeter of Figure 6 is **24**. The pattern in the table shows that the perimeter goes up in increments of 4 each time the figure number goes up by 1. Since the perimeter of Figure 5 is 20, the perimeter of Figure 6 is 24.

Figure number	Perimeter
1	4 >4
2	8 >4
3	12 >4
4	16 >4
5	20 >4
6	24

3. To make Figure 7, students need 70 toothpicks. The table shows that the total number of toothpicks in the design goes up by 2 more than the previous increase. Since the total number of toothpicks in Figure 5 is 40; the number for Figure 6 is 54 (an increase of 14); and thus, the number for Figure 7 is 70 (an increase of 16).

Figure number	Total toothpicks
1	4 > 6 >2
2	10 > 8 >2
3	18 > 10 >2
4	28 > 12 >2
5	40 > 14 >2
6	54 > 16 >2
7	70

Another way to think about the total number of toothpicks needed to make Figure 7 is to look at the toothpicks that need to be added to Figure 6. To add 7 boxes to Figure 6, one needs to add (2×8) or 16 toothpicks—8 horizontal toothpicks going from top to bottom, plus 7 toothpicks on the right and 1 toothpick on the left.

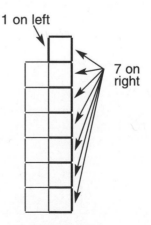

1 on left

7 on right

4. If P is the perimeter of Figure N, then: **$P = 4N.$**

5. If T is the total number of toothpicks needed to make Figure N, then:
$T = N^2 + 3N.$

6. The growth of the perimeter is **linear.** Its value increases at a constant rate. Also, if students graph the values for N (figure number) and P (the corresponding perimeter) and then connect the points, they would get a line.

7. The growth in the total number of toothpicks is **quadratic.** The value goes up at a constantly increasing rate. If students graph the values for N (figure number) and T (the corresponding total number of toothpicks) and then connect the points, they would get a parabola, an increasing curve, that indicates a quadratic relationship.

8. This question asks students to create their own toothpick design. To successfully complete all parts of the question, they need to choose a design whose perimeter and total number of toothpicks grow according to a fairly straightforward functional behavior. Otherwise, it could be very difficult to determine the rules requested in 8b and 8c. The following are two possible solutions.

Design A
b. $P = 2(N + 1) = 2N + 2$
c. $T = 4 + 3(N - 1) = 3N + 1$

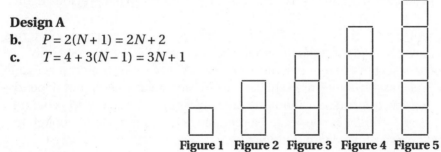

Figure 1 Figure 2 Figure 3 Figure 4 Figure 5

Design B
b. $P = 4N$
c. $T = 2N^2 + 2N$ **or** $2N(N + 1)$

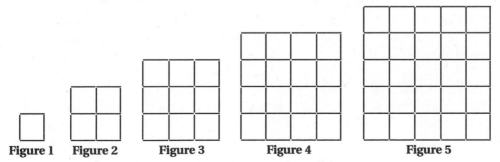

Figure 1   Figure 2   Figure 3   Figure 4   Figure 5

Task

More on the Mathematics

This task asks students to notice and generalize patterns. The patterns in this task are quite interesting and not obviously explainable. You may wish to encourage students to explore *why* the relationships they notice occur. How do their formulas fit with the changes in the actual figures? How can students be sure they will accurately predict values for additional figures that are not drawn? The following discussion offers some explanations about why some of the relationships that arise in this task occur.

In questions 2 and 3, students are asked to notice patterns of growth for both perimeter and total number of toothpicks. They are also asked to notice relationships in questions 4 and 5 between the numbers of the figures and their perimeters and between the numbers of the figures and the total number of toothpicks needed to make them.

When students focus on the growth of the numerical values in their tables, they tend to see the patterns *recursively*. This means that they notice how the patterns change from one figure to the next. For example, with perimeter growth, students may express this pattern symbolically as: "Perimeter = perimeter of the last figure + 4." Using more standard mathematical symbols, this may be expressed as $P_N = P_{N-1} + 4$ where P_N is the perimeter of Figure N and P_{N-1} is the perimeter of the previous figure.

Students may write their formula for the perimeter of the Figure N in terms of N. With such a formula, to find the perimeter of Figure 100, one only needs to plug in the number 100 in place of N. To be considered successful with this task, students are expected to offer formulas that do not depend on knowing information about the previous figure. Being able to generate recursive formulas is considered a productive step, but it is not enough to *meet the essential demands of the task.*

To see why the perimeter is always four times the figure number ($P = 4N$), we can look at the figures in this way. For any figure, you can "see" the entire perimeter by taking four views of the figure—top, bottom, left, and right. In each view, you see the number of toothpicks equal to the number of the figure. Since there are four views, the entire perimeter is 4 times the number of the figure.

To understand why the formula for total toothpicks is $T = N^2 + 3N$, turn to the construction of the figures. The total number of toothpicks needed to make Figure N includes its perimeter or $4N$. The "internal" number of toothpicks in Figure N is $N(N-1)$. We get this amount by adding the internal vertical toothpicks and the internal horizontal toothpicks. For example, with Figure 5, note that from the top, the internal vertical toothpicks are $1 + 2 + 3 + 4$. The same is true for the internal horizontal toothpicks. If we extend this reasoning to Figure N, the sum of the internal vertical toothpicks is $1 + 2 + \ldots + (N-1)$. The formula for finding this sum is $\frac{N(N-1)}{2}$. The sum of the internal horizontal toothpicks is also $1 + 2 + \ldots + (N-1)$ or $\frac{N(N-1)}{2}$. Taking the two sums together, we get $\frac{N(N-1)}{2} + \frac{N(N-1)}{2} = N(N-1)$, the sum of the internal toothpicks. We add the sums of the internal and perimeter toothpicks and simplify:

$$T = 4N + N(N-1)$$
$$T = 4N + N^2 - N$$
$$T = N^2 + 3N$$

The following are explanations for the formulas for the two sample figures given for question 8.

Design A

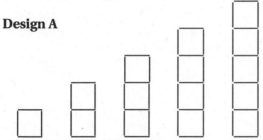

Figure 1   Figure 2   Figure 3   Figure 4   Figure 5

For any Figure N, there are N boxes. The length of each side is N or $2N$ for both sides. Then 2 more toothpicks are needed for top and bottom. So $P = 2N + 2$.

For any Figure N, the bottom box is made with 4 toothpicks. Each subsequent box requires 3 more toothpicks for $N-1$ total boxes. So $T = 4 + 3(N-1) = 3N + 1$.

Design B

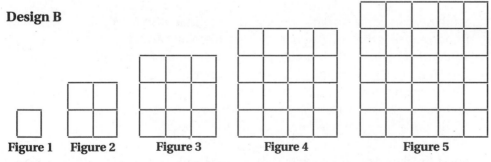

Figure 1   Figure 2   Figure 3   Figure 4   Figure 5

For any Figure N, the shape of the Figure is $N \times N$. So there are N toothpicks on each edge or 4 times N for all the edges. So the perimeter is given by $P = 4N$.

For any Figure N, there are N rows of N boxes. For the horizontal toothpicks, you need N toothpicks $N + 1$ times going from top to bottom. For the vertical toothpicks, you also need N toothpicks $N + 1$ times going from left to right. So you need $2N(N + 1)$ toothpicks in all. So $T = 2N(N + 1)$.

Task 1 Using this Task

For Formal Assessment

Hand out the task to students and review the aims of the assessment at the top of the first activity page. Read the problem aloud. Make sure that students understand that the designs depicted are made up of toothpicks. You may wish to demonstrate this with some toothpicks on an overhead projector. If students ask questions about what design to choose for the last question, tell them it is their choice. You can remind them that they should investigate a design that will allow them to answer all the questions (8a, b, and c) and that a design that grows in a very systematic way is needed to show patterns of change.

Issues for Classroom Use

The last question of this task asks students to create their own toothpick design and to determine general rules for finding the perimeter and the number of toothpicks needed to make any figure of their design. Students may choose designs that make it very difficult to find general rules. Such designs are often of the type that it may be obvious to the designing student how the design changes as it grows, but the change is not completely precise (for example, you add a box each time, but you could reasonably add it in more than one specific spot). Some students may need encouragement to try another design if "it doesn't work" to generalize rules for their first choice.

Students can come up with very creative original designs. Again, it is important that the designs increase systematically and that students remember their designs are made from toothpicks of fixed length. For example, while a student may devise a pattern using right triangles, the design will contain gaps and measures, such a perimeter, could differ from those of the same design made from a continuous material, such as string. In other words, students could possibly be mislead into thinking that their use of only one toothpick to make the hypotenuse of a right triangle means that the length of the hypotenuse is one toothpick. Here is an example of a "misleading" design. Note how the "toothpicks" cannot all be of the same length.

You may wish to extend this task by having students share their different toothpick designs with each other and the rules they found. Have students continue to create and explore different designs and take note of the functional behavior of perimeter and total toothpicks for each. Have students attempt to generalize about the kinds of designs that exhibit different kinds of functional behavior. What kinds of designs do not have rules that are easily generalized? What kinds of designs have linear growth in total toothpicks? Quadratic? Why do you think so?

You can also extend this task by having students explore *why* the generalizations they found for perimeter and total number of toothpicks work and attempt to "prove" them by referring back to the figures. Such kinds of explanations are given in **More on the Mathematics** at the end of the **Sample Solution** section.

Task 1 Characterizing Performance

This section offers a characterization of student responses and provides indications of the ways in which the students were successful or unsuccessful in engaging with and completing the task. The descriptions are keyed to the *Core Elements of Performance.* Our global descriptions of student work range from "The student needs significant instruction" to "The student's work meets the essential demands of the task." Samples of student work that exemplify these descriptions of performance are included below, accompanied by commentary on central aspects of each student's response. These sample responses are *representative;* they may not mirror the global description of performance in all respects, being weaker in some and stronger in others.

The characterization of student responses for this task is based on these *Core Elements of Performance:*
1. Extend patterns to find values for additional figures.
2. Use numerical and/or visual reasoning to find and symbolically describe rules.
3. Identify functional behavior and justify choice.
4. Create and generalize rules for their own growing toothpick design.

Descriptions of Student Work

The student needs significant instruction.

Student engages in the task and may find correct values for questions 1, 2, and 3 by extending the pattern and counting, but student does not demonstrate an ability to generalize about the functional relationships either in words or in symbols.

Student A

Student A shows some understanding of how the design changes as it grows. She successfully extends the pattern and finds correct answers to questions 2 and 3. However, she does so only by counting toothpicks and shows no understanding of the functional relationships involved, how to generalize them, nor how to predict values for additional figures without drawing them. With her original toothpick design, Student A again shows an understanding of consistently growing patterns, but does not talk about relationships between the figures and their perimeters nor the number of toothpicks needed to make them.

The student needs some instruction.

Student gives generalizations in words and/or symbols for the functional relationships in the task, but does so only recursively or gives a formula for perimeter only that does not depend on the previous figure. Student may or may not show some success with other aspects of the task.

Student B

Student B shows that he is generalizing about the numerical patterns of growth of perimeter and total number of toothpicks in both his written explanations in questions 2 and 3 and in his formulas. However, he is only viewing the patterns recursively. He also fails to clearly express them symbolically. Student B does not construct a design with a consistent growth pattern in question 8 and his generalizations do not correspond to the figures shown.

Student C

Student C describes perimeter growth recursively in question 2, but gives a formula in question 4. In question 3, she determines the total number of toothpicks by drawing the figure and counting, but in question 5, she presents a formula that describes a relationship she noticed. To use this formula, one must have a drawing of the figure and count the number of "blocks" it contains. Student C's formula cannot determine the total number of toothpicks needed to make some arbitrary Figure N independent of a drawing or more information about the figure.

The student's work needs to be revised.

Student provides generalizations that do not depend on information about the previous picture in words and/or symbols for both perimeter and total number of toothpicks for the given and/or for an original design, but student fails to successfully complete one or more parts of the task.
That is, student does not show an understanding of how to characterize the functional relationships (does not correctly answer questions 6 and 7); does not successfully create and find generalizations for an original toothpick design (does not correctly and completely answer question 8); and/or the student expresses reasoning poorly (does not offer justifications in a number of questions: 2, 3, 6, and/or 7, and he/she does not identify variables, and so on).

Task

1

Student D

Student D gives correct generalizations in questions 8b and 8c, but not in question 5. In all his formulas, however, it is not completely clear what his variables represent. He states that S is the "number of squares," but if this is the case, his formula in question 4 does not work, but it does work if S is the figure number. Student D correctly identifies functional behavior in questions 6 and 7 and gives sufficient justifications even though he is not able to come up with the generalizations in question 5.

The student's work meets the essential demands of the task.

Student provides symbolic generalizations for both perimeter and total number of toothpicks that are not dependent on knowing information about the previous figure, provides correct answers and justifications in questions 2, 3, 6, and 7, AND student successfully creates and provides symbolic generalizations not dependent on the previous figure for an original toothpick design. (Some errors or weaknesses that do not reflect a failure to meet the essence of the *Core Elements of Performance* are permitted.)

Student E

Student E answers all questions in the task correctly. She provides justifications where asked and gives correct formulas for perimeter and total number of toothpicks for both the given design and for her original one. Student E's explanations in questions 6 and 7 show basic ideas with no elaboration.

Toothpicks

This problem gives you the chance to

- *investigate, extend, symbolically generalize, and create patterns*
- *use numerical and/or visual reasoning*
- *discuss functional behavior*

The figures shown below are made with toothpicks.

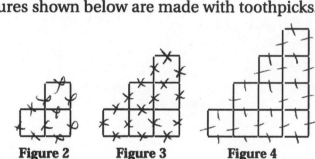

Figure 1   Figure 2   Figure 3   Figure 4   Figure 5

1. Make a table to the right showing:
   a. the number of the figure
   b. the perimeter of the figure (in number of toothpicks)
   c. the total number of toothpicks (needed to make the figure)

Figure 1	Figure 2	Figure 3	Figure 4	Figure 5
Perimeter 4	8	12	16	20
total toth 4	10	18	26	40

2. Extending the pattern, what is the perimeter of **Figure 6**?

   Show or explain how you figured this out.
   24 Added one more block to the bottom and one in the height

3. How many toothpicks are needed to make **Figure 7**? Show or

   explain how you figured this out. 70 Added two to the bottom of Figure 6 and two to the top of figure 6 and counted the lines.

4. Write a formula that could be used to find the **perimeter** of any Figure *N*. Tell what your variables represent.

N + Number of blocks being Added.

5. Write a formula that could be used to find the **total number of toothpicks** needed to make any Figure *N*. Tell what your variables represent.

L x W

6. Is the growth of the **perimeter** linear, quadratic, or exponential? Give reasons for your decision.

Linear because you Are Adding things to A line or colemn

7. Is the growth of the **total number of toothpicks** linear, quadratic, or exponential? Give reasons for your decision.

Quadratic because here you Are Adding All Around in A square shape A quadratic figure.

8. Create your own toothpick pattern.

   a. Show at least **5** different figures of your pattern that show how the figure changes as it grows. Make sure it is clear how to continue your pattern.

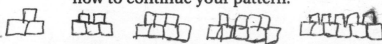

   b. Write an equation or rule that could be used to find the **perimeter** of any size of your design (Figure *N*).

Every time you Add one to the bottom one Adds to the top.

   c. Write an equation or rule that could be used to find **the total number of toothpicks** needed for any size of your design (Figure *N*).

add All the toothpicks but relize that sometimes A toothpick is shared or halfs Are Put tusether for one whole

Student B

Toothpicks

This problem gives you the chance to

- *investigate, extend, symbolically generalize, and create patterns*
- *use numerical and/or visual reasoning*
- *discuss functional behavior*

The figures shown below are made with toothpicks.

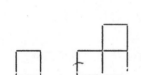 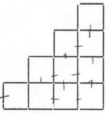 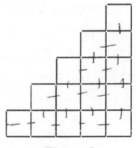

Figure 1   **Figure 2**   **Figure 3**   **Figure 4**   **Figure 5**

1. Make a table to the right showing:

   a. the number of the figure

   b. the perimeter of the figure (in number of toothpicks)

   c. the total number of toothpicks (needed to make the figure)

2. Extending the pattern, what is the perimeter of **Figure 6**? Show or explain how you figured this out.   24

   I figured this out because the pattern ~~its to add~~ 4 every time.

3. How many toothpicks are needed to make **Figure 7**? Show or explain how you figured this out.   54

   you add 2 more than you did last time.

4. Write a formula that could be used to find the **perimeter** of any Figure *N*. Tell what your variables represent.

$$n + 4$$

5. Write a formula that could be used to find the **total number of toothpicks** needed to make any Figure *N*. Tell what your variables represent.

$$n + 2 \text{ more than previous}$$

6. Is the growth of the **perimeter** linear, quadratic, or exponential? Give reasons for your decision. ~~quadratic~~ exponential

Because you add ~~two~~ toothpicks every time.

7. Is the growth of the **total number of toothpicks** linear, quadratic, or exponential? Give reasons for your decision. ~~quadratic~~

~~Because you add four toothpicks every time.~~

8. Create your own toothpick pattern.

   a. Show at least **5** different figures of your pattern that show how the figure changes as it grows. Make sure it is clear how to continue your pattern.

   b. Write an equation or rule that could be used to find the **perimeter** of any size of your design (Figure *N*).

   $$n + 3$$

   c. Write an equation or rule that could be used to find **the total number of toothpicks** needed for any size of your design (Figure *N*).

   $$n + 1 \text{ more than previous}$$

Student C

Toothpicks

This problem gives you the chance to

■ *investigate, extend, symbolically generalize, and create patterns*

■ *use numerical and/or visual reasoning*

■ *discuss functional behavior*

The figures shown below are made with toothpicks.

Figure 1   Figure 2   Figure 3   Figure 4   Figure 5

1. Make a table to the right showing:
   a. the number of the figure
   b. the perimeter of the figure (in number of toothpicks)
   c. the total number of toothpicks (needed to make the figure)

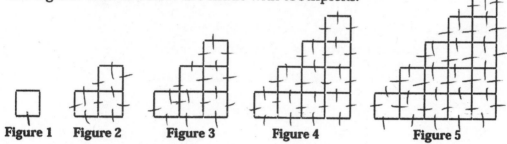

figure #	1	2	3	4	5
Perimeter (toothpicks)	4	8	12	16	20
total # of toothpicks	4	10	18	28	40

2. Extending the pattern, what is the perimeter of **Figure 6?**
   Show or explain how you figured this out. Perimeter of figure 6 is 24 Because the numbers grow by 4 each time

3. How many toothpicks are needed to make **Figure 7?** Show or explain how you figured this out. total number of toothpicks is 70

4. Write a formula that could be used to find the **perimeter** of any Figure *N*. Tell what your variables represent.

$$P = N4$$

5. Write a formula that could be used to find the **total number of toothpicks** needed to make any Figure *N*. Tell what your variables represent.

total number of toothpicks = (total blocks × 3) + 1

6. Is the growth of the **perimeter** linear, quadratic, or exponential? Give reasons for your decision.

linear because it grows at the same rate

7. Is the growth of the **total number of toothpicks** linear, quadratic, or exponential? Give reasons for your decision.

exponential, because it has an exponential growth pattern

8. Create your own toothpick pattern.

   a. Show at least **5** different figures of your pattern that show how the figure changes as it grows. Make sure it is clear how to continue your pattern.

   b. Write an equation or rule that could be used to find the **perimeter** of any size of your design (Figure *N*).

   P = p from previous figure + 2

   c. Write an equation or rule that could be used to find **the total number of toothpicks** needed for any size of your design (Figure *N*).

   Toothpicks = (#B × 3) + 1

Student D

Toothpicks

This problem gives you the chance to

- *investigate, extend, symbolically generalize, and create patterns*
- *use numerical and/or visual reasoning*
- *discuss functional behavior*

The figures shown below are made with toothpicks.

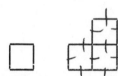 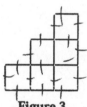 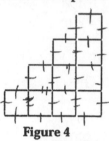 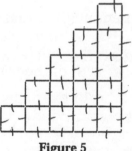

Figure 1   **Figure 2**   **Figure 3**   **Figure 4**   **Figure 5**

1. Make a table to the right showing:

   a. the number of the figure

   b. the perimeter of the figure (in number of toothpicks)

   c. the total number of toothpicks (needed to make the figure)

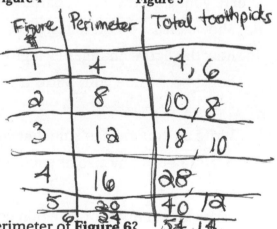

Figure #	Perimeter	Total toothpicks
1	4	4, 6
2	8	10, 8
3	12	18, 10
4	16	28
5	20 24	40 12
6		54, 14

2. Extending the pattern, what is the perimeter of **Figure 6**? Show or explain how you figured this out.

   4 - 8 - 12 - 16 - 20 (it goes by 4.)
   24 toothpicks

3. How many toothpicks are needed to make **Figure 7**? Show or explain how you figured this out. 4 - 10 - 18 - 28 - 40 is in increments increasing by 2. Last increment was 12 so 6 would be 14 and 7 would be 16

   70 toothpicks

4. Write a formula that could be used to find the **perimeter** of any Figure *N*. Tell what your variables represent.

Number of Sqaures (S)
P= Perimeter   S4=P

5. Write a formula that could be used to find the **total number of toothpicks** needed to make any Figure *N*. Tell what your variables represent.

4+(s-1)2

6. Is the growth of the **perimeter** linear, quadratic, or exponential? Give reasons for your decision.

The growth of the perimeter is linear, because it increases at a steady rate of 4.

7. Is the growth of the **total number of toothpicks** linear, quadratic, or exponential? Give reasons for your decision.

The growth of the total number of toothpicks is quadratic, because it doesn't increase at a steady rate, but it doesn't increase at a multiplying rat, so it can't be exponential.

8. Create your own toothpick pattern.

   a. Show at least **5** different figures of your pattern that show how the figure changes as it grows. Make sure it is clear how to continue your pattern.

   b. Write an equation or rule that could be used to find the **perimeter** of any size of your design (Figure *N*).

4+(S-1)2 = Perimeter

   c. Write an equation or rule that could be used to find **the total number of toothpicks** needed for any size of your design (Figure *N*).

4+(s-1)3 = Total toothpicks

Toothpicks

This problem gives you the chance to

- *investigate, extend, symbolically generalize, and create patterns*
- *use numerical and/or visual reasoning*
- *discuss functional behavior*

The figures shown below are made with toothpicks.

 4

 10

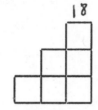 18

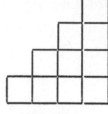 28

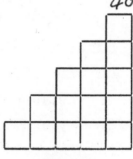 40

Figure 1   Figure 2   Figure 3   Figure 4   Figure 5

1. Make a table to the right showing:
   a. the number of the figure
   b. the perimeter of the figure (in number of toothpicks)
   c. the total number of toothpicks (needed to make the figure)

n(n+3)

#Figure	Perimeter	Total
1	4	4
2	8	10
3	12	18
4	16	28
5	20	40

→6 ⟩2
→8 ⟩2
→10 ⟩2
→12

2. Extending the pattern, what is the perimeter of **Figure 6**? Show or explain how you figured this out. 24. Rule= P=4f

p= perimeter
f= figure #

3. How many toothpicks are needed to make **Figure 7**? Show or explain how you figured this out. The change is 2 more each time, so you would add 14 and then 16 to figure 5! ⑦⓪

4. Write a formula that could be used to find the **perimeter** of any Figure *N*. Tell what your variables represent.

$P = 4n$ p= perimeter
n= figure number

5. Write a formula that could be used to find the **total number of toothpicks** needed to make any Figure *N*. Tell what your variables represent.

n= figure #
$T = n(n+3)$ or $n^2 + 3n$ t= total # toothpicks

6. Is the growth of the **perimeter** linear, quadratic, or exponential? Give reasons for your decision.

Linear. It has no exponents.

7. Is the growth of the **total number of toothpicks** linear, quadratic, or exponential? Give reasons for your decision.

Quadratic. It's n squared.

8. Create your own toothpick pattern.

 a. Show at least **5** different figures of your pattern that show how the figure changes as it grows. Make sure it is clear how to continue your pattern.

   See back of p. 1.

 b. Write an equation or rule that could be used to find the **perimeter** of any size of your design (Figure *N*).

   $P = 2n + 2$

 c. Write an equation or rule that could be used to find **the total number of toothpicks** needed for any size of your design (Figure *N*).

   $4 + 3(n-1)$

8. Figure 1   Figure 2   Figure 3

Figure 4   Figure 5

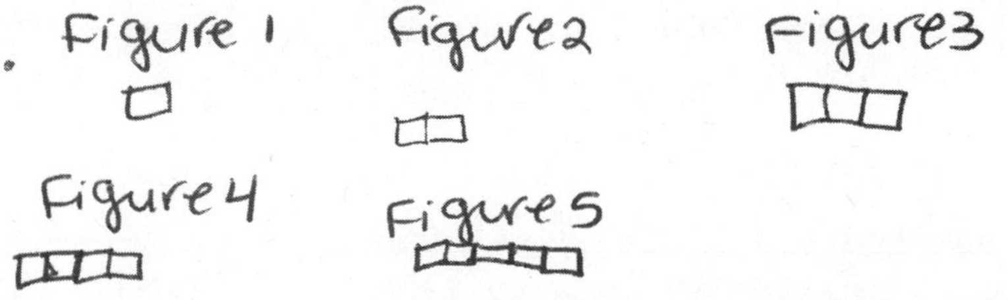

Camp Placement

Long Task

Task Description

Students are given numerical and descriptive data on twelve campers. They must organize the campers into three groups. Students are to decide on the purpose of the groups, use the given information to form the groups, and then justify their selection.

Assumed Mathematical Background

It is assumed that students have had experience with analyzing and interpreting data that involve several variables.

Core Elements of Performance

- select a reasonable context for pursuing the task
- analyze and interpret data from multiple variables to form groups
- justify selection process and resultant groups, based on data analysis

Circumstances

Grouping:	Students may discuss the task in pairs and complete a combined written response.
Materials:	No special materials are needed for this task.
Estimated time:	45 minutes

Acknowledgment

We thank the Applied Problem Solving Project for their work on this task.

Camp Placement

This problem gives you the chance to
- *analyze and interpret data*
- *justify a decision based on the data analysis*

With a partner

Imagine that you are one of three counselors at a sports camp specializing in track and field. Preliminary events are held during the first day of camp. Since the camp is located on a lake, the campers' swimming skills are recorded along with their track-and-field results. The 12-year-old boys performed as follows:

Name	50-meter Run (sec.)	100-meter Run (sec.)	High Jump	Long Jump	Swim Level*
Andy	7.9	14.6	4' 2"	10' 9"	Bass
Brian	9.4	16.5	3' 4"	10' 0"	Sunfish
Charles	7.0	13.5	4' 4"	11' 6"	Shark
Doug	7.8	14.4	4' 7"	12' 0"	Bass
Eric	6.8	12.6	4' 8"	12' 2"	Shark
Fred	8.0	14.5	4' 1"	10' 9"	Trout
Greg	8.1	15.0	4' 3"	10' 6"	Trout
Herb	7.2	13.8	4' 3"	9' 3"	Shark
John	7.7	14.0	4' 4"	10' 11"	Trout
Kevin	7.4	14.0	3' 8"	11' 2"	Bass
Larry	7.7	14.2	4' 6"	11' 0"	Bass
Mike	8.0	15.0	4' 0"	10' 2"	Trout

*Swim levels, from highest to lowest, are Shark, Bass, Trout, and Sunfish.

Before camp begins, a letter is sent to the track-and-field coach at each boy's school. The coaches are asked to give information about the boys that would be helpful to the camp counselors. The following comments were sent to the camp.

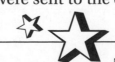

© *The Regents of the University of California*

Coaches' Comments

Andy: Tremendous effort has helped Andy make some good gains this season, but his performance is not consistent.

Brian: An unwillingness to follow team rules, and goofing around during practice have surely contributed to Brian's deplorable performance.

Charles: He has consistently worked hard.

Doug: Doug has good endurance in most running events, but his performance in some throwing events tends to be sloppy.

Eric: Eric is a dedicated and motivated team member.

Fred: Fair ability in most events does not offset Fred's poor attitude toward practice.

Greg: Immature behavior has interfered with his progress this year and he has occasionally disrupted the whole group. Greg seems to do the least work required to stay on our track team.

Herb: Herb has shown tremendous improvement this year. His previous training had been rather weak, so he still has a lot to learn.

John: John has a lot of natural athletic ability but hasn't worked up to his potential because of missed practice and failure to pay attention to advice during practice.

Kevin: He is a natural athlete who hasn't worked up to his potential. I think Kevin needs more of a challenge, more competition, to make him work harder.

Larry: Larry is a rather shy boy who doesn't care to be in the spotlight. He just doesn't seem comfortable with heavy competition.

Mike: Although Mike's ability in jumping events is not outstanding, he has made good progress this year in sprinting.

Based on the preceding information, you are to assign these twelve campers into three groups. You will need to write a report that includes the following information:

- Decide and explain the purpose for your groupings.
- List the students that are grouped together.
- Justify your decision for assigning campers into their groups.

© The Regents of the University of California

Task

A Sample Solution

Sample Solution A
The following sample response explains the advantages to homogeneous grouping.

We decided to place the campers in groups for the purpose of practicing and improving their track-and-field skills. We wanted to put campers of similar ability together, but wanted to avoid having too many campers with poor attitudes in the same group. We thought that if campers within the same group share similar abilities, they would compete against each other and improve. We also didn't want any of the boys in a group to feel that they were worse off than any of the others in the group because we feared that they would stop trying.

Since swimming is not part of track and field, we looked only at the data on campers' running times, jumping heights and distances, and their coaches' comments. We ranked campers in each of the four relevant events (bold numbers). The campers we underlined were reported as having poor attitudes and having the potential to disrupt the group.

Name	50-meter Run (sec.)		100-meter Run (sec.)		High Jump		Long Jump	
Andy	7.9	**8**	14.6	**9**	4' 2"	**8**	10' 9"	**7**
Brian	9.4	**12**	16.5	**12**	3' 4"	**12**	10' 0"	**11**
Charles	7.0	**2**	13.5	**2**	4' 4"	**4**	11' 6"	**3**
Doug	7.8	**7**	14.4	**7**	4' 7"	**2**	12' 0"	**2**
Eric	6.8	**1**	12.6	**1**	4' 8"	**1**	12' 2"	**1**
Fred	8.0	**9**	14.5	**8**	4' 1"	**9**	10' 9"	**7**
Greg	8.1	**11**	15.0	**10**	4' 3"	**6**	10' 6"	**9**
Herb	7.2	**3**	13.8	**3**	4' 3"	**6**	9' 3"	**12**
John	7.7	**5**	14.0	**4**	4' 4"	**4**	10' 11"	**6**
Kevin	7.4	**4**	14.0	**4**	3' 8"	**11**	11' 2"	**4**
Larry	7.7	**5**	14.2	**6**	4' 6"	**3**	11' 0"	**5**
Mike	8.0	**9**	15.0	**10**	4' 0"	**10**	10' 2"	**10**

Groups:

High ability	Medium ability	Low ability
Eric	Doug	Brian
Charles	Herb	Mike
Kevin	Larry	Andy
John	Fred	Greg

We first assigned Eric and Charles to the high-ability group since they were clearly the best athletes. We also put Kevin in the high group since he ranked fourth in three events. He could have just screwed up in high jump. Also his coach said that he needs more competition to improve. We put John in the high-ability group because he did consistently well on all events. Also, although John is not really a troublemaker, his coach said that he doesn't listen to advice, so he would probably benefit from the good attitudes of the other campers in the high group.

Doug, Larry, and Herb went into the medium-ability group. They all performed very well on one or two events (within the top third of the campers), but need work on other events. Andy seems to rank a little higher than Fred in ability, but because Fred needs work on his attitude, we decided to put him in this group.

It was easy to assign Brian and Mike to the low-ability group since they ranked in the bottom third of the campers in all events. Greg is also a poor performer and has a poor attitude like Brian, but we hope that the positive attitudes of Mike and Andy will help him stay focused.

Sample Solution B
The following sample response explains the advantages to heterogeneous grouping.

The purpose of the groups is for the campers to participate as part of a team in camp competitions. Each group will be a team and the teams will compete against each other. We wanted to make the teams as fair as possible, so that each one has a chance of winning and the competition feels real. We also wanted the teams to be balanced in both ability and attitude.

To find the campers' relative abilities, we ranked them according to their times and distances on the running and jumping events (rankings are the bold numbers). We also underlined the names of the campers with the worse attitudes to make sure we separate them.

Task 2

Name	50-meter Run (sec.)		100-meter Run (sec.)		High Jump		Long Jump		Swim Level
Andy	7.9	8	14.6	9	4' 2"	8	10' 9"	7	Bass
Brian	9.4	12	16.5	12	3' 4"	12	10' 0"	11	Sunfish
Charles	7.0	2	13.5	2	4' 4"	4	11' 6"	3	Shark
Doug	7.8	7	14.4	7	4' 7"	2	12' 0"	2	Bass
Eric	6.8	1	12.6	1	4' 8"	1	12' 2"	1	Shark
Fred	8.0	9	14.5	8	4' 1"	9	10' 9"	7	Trout
Greg	8.1	11	15.0	10	4' 3"	6	10' 6"	9	Trout
Herb	7.2	3	13.8	3	4' 3"	6	9' 3"	12	Shark
John	7.7	5	14.0	4	4' 4"	4	10' 11"	6	Trout
Kevin	7.4	4	14.0	4	3' 8"	11	11' 2"	4	Bass
Larry	7.7	5	14.2	6	4' 6"	3	11' 0"	5	Bass
Mike	8.0	9	15.0	10	4' 0"	10	10' 2"	10	Trout

Using this information, we made the following teams:

Team 1	Team 2	Team 3
Eric	Charles	Kevin
Greg	Brian	Fred
John	Larry	Herb
Mike	Andy	Doug

We split up Eric, Charles, and Kevin since they are three of the top all-around athletes. Although Kevin's scores are the lowest of the three, his coach says that he does not perform at his full potential. Perhaps by competing with Eric and Charles and being the lead athlete on his team, Kevin will be motivated to work harder.

We split up Brian, Greg, and Fred since they are the campers who have the most destructive attitudes. They also are among the poorest athletes. Since Fred seems to be the best all-around athlete of these three (though not by much), we decided to place him with Kevin.

John, Larry, and Herb are each pretty consistent middling athletes, so we put one of them on each team. Since Herb is a good runner, but not such a good jumper, we matched him with Doug who has the opposite skills. Andy and Mike are among the poorer athletes but have very good attitudes and show potential for improvement, so we put each one on a team that still needed a member.

Using this Task

Discuss with students what they know about track and field and the events that make up the sport. Students do not need a complete understanding of the sport to engage in this task. However, students *do* need to understand that in running events, the lowest times win, and in jumping events, highest and furthest jumps win.

Once students understand the context of the task, read the aims of the assessment in the box at the top of the first activity page. Read through the task directions (above the numerical data, below the numerical data, and at the end of the task). Ask students how many different kinds of data are given. Emphasize that students are to consider all the data that are relevant to the purpose of their groups. In justifying their decision for assigning campers to groups, remind students that they must be clear about what data they used and how they used them. For example, you may reiterate the directions by saying, "Don't just say 'these campers have the highest ability' or 'these other campers need extra encouragement.' Explain how you decided to group them as you did. Write about the data. Explain how the data relate to your decisions."

You can bring up other examples of grouping people and how one might establish criteria for assigning people to groups, but try not to lead students into a specific direction, such as in thinking about ability grouping alone. For example, suppose the class was going on a field trip and half the class would go to the science museum and the other half to the history museum. How could the teacher decide who in the class should go to each museum? (Answers could be based on student requests, student interest in science or history, student achievement in these subjects, a need to increase student enthusiasm in these subjects, and so on.)

Issues for Classroom Use

Students seem to have little difficulty understanding the context of this task and in forming groups of campers for a specific, chosen purpose. Students do struggle with justifying their decisions on the basis of data analysis. The data in this task are deliberately messy. Depending on the purpose of their groups, students do not need to consider all of the data, but they should consider multiple variables. Students may also feel that the data are insufficient for their purpose (for example, they may want information on additional events such as shot put or discus throw distances or more detailed comments from coaches). One of the purposes of this task is to have students sift through messy data and develop schemes for organizing and making sense of it, as well as to decide what data to consider. This task also gives students the opportunity to experience a decision-making process based on a limited amount of information.

Task **Characterizing Performance**

This section offers a characterization of student responses and provides indications of the ways in which the students were successful or unsuccessful in engaging with and completing the task. The descriptions are keyed to the *Core Elements of Performance.* Our global descriptions of student work range from "The student needs significant instruction" to "The student's work meets the essential demands of the task." Samples of student work that exemplify these descriptions of performance are included below, accompanied by commentary on central aspects of each student's response. These sample responses are *representative;* they may not mirror the global description of performance in all respects, being weaker in some and stronger in others.

The characterization of student responses for this task is based on these *Core Elements of Performance:*

1. Select a reasonable context for pursuing the task.
2. Analyze and interpret data from multiple variables to form groups.
3. Justify selection process and resultant groups, based on data analysis.

Descriptions of Student Work

The group needs significant instruction.

These groups form three arrangements of campers, but with no apparent system or a system that is unreasonable to the general context of track and field or not clearly linked to any of the variables.

Group A

Group A states that they want "the right combination" and claim that they looked at ability and attitude to arrange their groups. They also say they "want them to improve, this is the purpose for the groups." They do not, however, explain how they decided who needed to improve nor do they explain which ability needs improvement. Their purpose is especially confusing given the names of their groups. For example, does the "sprint" group consist of campers who are good sprinters, who need to work on sprinting, or something else entirely? There is no explanation as to how their decisions relate to the given data.

Group B

Group B does not express a clear purpose for their groups (all they say is "by the ability"). Although they use a clear system, the system is unreasonable. The students added all the times and distances for each camper together. This means that they ignored the different referents of the numbers and also treated 4'2" as 4.2, which is incorrect. While the students seem to recognize (in their final paragraph) that it does not make sense to add high jumping scores with low running scores, they do not change their system.

The group needs some instruction.

Groups use a clear system to place the campers into groups, but the system is linked to only one variable *AND* the justification is weak, inconsistent, or unclear.

Group C

Group C uses a system that only considers the coaches' comments. Although they say they looked at performance as well, they show no evidence of this in their groupings. For example, for their second group, the students say the campers all "had strong points in certain events." They placed Mike in this group and although Mike's coach says, "he has made good progress this year in sprinting," times in running events and distances in jumping events placed him consistently in the lower third of the campers. The group's justification is somewhat unclear and inconsistent. They do not directly justify any of their characterizations of the campers and thus seem to place them inconsistently. For example, Andy is in the troublesome group, but his coach made no comments to this effect.

The group's work needs to be revised.

Students in these groups create a system that relies on only one variable or only on nonnumerical data *BUT* justification is strong *OR* students consider multiple variables in forming groups of campers *AND* justification is weak, incomplete, or poorly expressed.

Group D

Group D shows in their groupings that they considered multiple variables— their choices of "moderate" and "good guys" are consistent with perfor- mance data and the "slackers" are in line with the coaches' comments. Had they not considered these multiple variables, they would not have formed the groups that they did. For example, the students consider Kevin a "real good guy." The performance data shows him as ranked fourth among the campers in three of the four track-and-field events, but his coach describes

Task

him as someone "who hasn't worked up to his potential." If they considered the coaches' comments alone, they may have placed Kevin with the slackers. Their selection according to these criteria (heterogeneous resultant groups) makes sense relative to their purpose of forming teams. Their justification, however, is incomplete.

The group's work meets the essential demands of the task.

The groups consider multiple variables (including at least one numeric variable) and reasonably assign campers to groups based on their system *AND* justification is strong.

Group E

Group E arranges campers homogeneously by ability and attitude and explains the purpose for this division. Group E seems to rely heavily on the coaches' comments and demonstrates consideration of performance in only a few places. However, they show consideration of multiple variables and give clear and thorough justification for each placement.

Sprints	Jumping	Swimming
Eric	Charles	Andy
Kevin	mike	Herb
Doug	fred	Brian
John	Greg	larry

The porpose for the groups was trying to get the right combination. To find the right combination we grouped people with there ability and there attitude. If people were really good at a sport but had a bad attitude then I would try to group them with people who had a really good attitude so that they would feel uncomfortable to being silly and then they would work harder and then improve. also we put people in groups that weren't as good at that sport. We want them to improve. this is the porpose for the groups.

Andy: Not consitant   Total
Brian: Slacker   37.6/B —
Charles: consitant   39.3/S —
Doug: 36.5/Sh —
Eric   38.9/B —
Fred   →37.5← 36.4/Sh —
Greg   38.0/T —
Herb   34.6/Sh —
John   36.2/T —
Kevin   36.4/B —
Larry   37.5/B —
Mike   37.2/T —

   We decided apon our groups by the ability that they showed
in the events listed on the pages given.

                                                    34.6
Group#1.   Herb   34.6   36.2
            Charles 36.5   36.4
            Andy   37.6   36.4
            Brian 39.3   36.5
                                                    37.2
                                                    37.5
Group#2.   John 36.2   37.5
            Mike 37.2   37.6
            Fred 37.5   38.0
             Greg 38.0   38.7
                                                    39.3

Group#2   Eric 36.4
            Kevin 36.4
            Larry 37.5
            Doug 38.9

   Our decision in making the groups we that we put same low
scores and some largh scores together, but the way that we did
it made it random because of the high jump.

We split the campers into three groups to do this we first looked at all of the kids track and field coaches comments. Then on the bases on their comments and the kids times we devided them into the groups. for the 1st group we took the kids with the best Attitudes, who Always worked hard and could handle a higher comptition. This group consisted of Charles, Eric, Fred, and Kevin.

for our second group we took the kids who had strong points in certain events, but still had a lot to learn. This group also showed positive attitudes but had more to work on to improve their track skills than the 1st group. This group consisted of Doug, Herb, Larry, and Mike.

The last group of kids were put togeather because of their poor attitudes, unwillingness to follow directions, advice, and rules. Also they showed unconsistent times in their events. This group consisted of Andy, Brian, Greg, and John.

we think that this was afair way to group the campers because of their coaches comments From previous years and their times and levels From the preliminary events held on the first day at camp.

Purpose for Groups - Divide *Slackers° Speed out real good guys so they can better team

Group 1	Group 2	Group 3
Brian	Greg	John
Eric	Charlie	Kevin
Andy	Doug	Herb
Mike	Fred	Larry

We put to Moderate Guys (Andy, Mike, Larry, Herb, Doug & Fred) wherever they fit.

We put the real good guys with the Slackers to ! Keep *slackers apart° Balance team out so two real good guys are together ³ to help *Slackers get motivated.

* Slacker - Some one who goofs off, Does minimal amount work, Doesn't pull own weight

The purpose for the different groups is to match the different campers up & put them in groups according to how well they perform, act, and their attitude. By doing this you could maybe help the students to do better in the areas they are weak in by working with them on a more individual basis.

(BEST)	(Middle)	(WORST)
- Group #1	Group #2	Group #3
1) ERiC	Herb	Brian
2) Charles	John	GreG
3) Andy	Fred	mike
4) Kevin	Doug	larry

For Group #1 we put the campers in it that we thought proformed well & has high expectations. We put ERiC in this groupe because he had the highest scores out of everyone & his report said that he is very dedicated & motivated team player. Charles was put in the group because he has pretty good scores & he werks really hard. Andy fits in to the 1st group because he puts effort in' & made some gains this season but eventhough he isn't very consistant. We thought that

If he's in a groupe w/ people more consistant than him, he can learn from his other group members. Kevin fits in because his report said that maybe if he was put with people that would give him more of a challenge he would perform better.

For the second group we picked people that would be in the middle of the students. Herb was picked because he has shown alot of improvement but he is weak so he can learn form his other group members. John goes in because he has a natural ability to proform but he doesn't attend practice regularly so he is in the middle. Fred fits in, he has a good attatude but fair ability. Doug, he could be helped on being more consistant.

For the third group Brian was picked because he goofs around alot, doesn't have good scores, & doesn't attend practice. Greg has immiture behavior. Mike, Needs to work on certain activities more. Larry, he doesn't handle competition very well so he should be put in a low group.

Matting a Photo

Long Task

Task Description

Students write directions on how to cut an opening for a $3\frac{1}{2}$-by-5-inch photo from a 5-by-7-inch rectangular matte board.

Assumed Mathematical Background

It is assumed that students have had some experience with calculation involving fractions and measurement.

Core Elements of Performance

- use visual reasoning, measurement, and calculations involving fractions to reason about rectangles in an applied setting

- write a clear and complete set of directions

Circumstances

Grouping:	Following some entry work in pairs, students complete an individual written response.
Materials:	inch rulers (marked to sixteenths of inches) and tape
Estimated time:	45 minutes

Matting a Photo

This problem gives you the chance to

- *use geometric and measurement ideas in an applied setting*
- *communicate mathematical ideas to an audience*

You and your partner have been hired by the Do-It-Yourself Frame Store to help customers matte their own pictures. A customer wants to matte a photograph that is a common size: $3\frac{1}{2}$ inches by 5 inches.

All mattes start off as a solid rectangular piece of cardboard. The one that would be used for this sized photograph measures 5 inches by 7 inches.

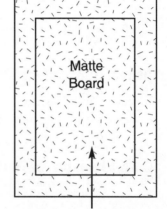

Cut a rectangular opening

A rectangular opening needs to be cut into the center of the matte to display the $3\frac{1}{2}$-by-5-inch picture, which is positioned behind the matte.

The opening in the matte needs to overlap the photo by $\frac{1}{8}$ to $\frac{1}{4}$ inch all the way around, so the photo edge will not slip out once the picture is framed.

Customers have access to rulers that measure to the nearest $\frac{1}{16}$ inch.

© The Regents of the University of California

With a partner

1. Write a first draft of very specific instructions that a customer could use to matte a $3\frac{1}{2}$-by-5-inch photo. Your instructions should include a diagram and they should be written for any customer who is matting a photo for the first time.

2. To test your instructions, follow them to matte the picture using the next two pages. Make notes of any problems with your instructions.

On your own

3. Write a final set of instructions. You may modify and refine your draft to make them as clear and specific as possible for customers. Remember, even new customers must be able to follow your set of instructions and they should include a diagram.

© The Regents of the University of California

Matte Board

© *The Regents of the University of California*

$3\frac{1}{2}$-by-5-inch picture

© The Regents of the University of California

Task **A Sample Solution**

First, to find out where to put the photo, compute the difference between the width of the matte and the width of the photo.

$$5 - 3\tfrac{1}{2} = 1\tfrac{1}{2} \text{ inches}$$

Now, you want this amount to be divided evenly on both sides of the photograph.

$$1\tfrac{1}{2} \div 2 = \tfrac{3}{4}$$

Add the $\tfrac{1}{4}$-inch overlap to get the final answer width of the matte on each side of the photo.

$$\tfrac{3}{4} + \tfrac{1}{4} = 1 \text{ inch}$$

Now you need to do the same thing to find the width of the matte at the top and bottom of the picture. Again, find the difference between the length of the picture and the length of the matte.

$$7 - 5 = 2 \text{ inches}$$

Now, you want this amount to be divided evenly on both sides of the photograph.

$$2 \div 2 = 1 \text{ inch}$$

Add the $\tfrac{1}{4}$-inch overlap to get the final answer for the width of the matte above and below the picture.

$$1 + \tfrac{1}{4} = 1\tfrac{1}{4} \text{ inches}$$

Now we need to cut the opening in the matte for the photo. Make the marks on the back of the matte so that they do not show when you are finished.

1. Measure in 1 inch from the 7-inch side of the matte. Mark this place with a dot.

2. Repeat this process on the same side of the matte but at a different point on the side.

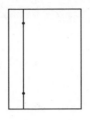

3. Draw a line through these two marks creating a line parallel to the edge of the matte.

4. Repeat the above steps on the opposite side of the matte.

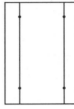

5. Now measure in $1\frac{1}{4}$ inches from the top of the matte and mark a dot.

6. Do this again at a different point from the top of the matte board.

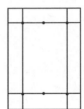

7. Draw the line connecting the dots.

8. Repeat this to draw a line $1\frac{1}{4}$ inches from the bottom of the matte.

9. Cut out the inside rectangle from the matte board.

10. From the opening that you have just cut out, measure in $\frac{1}{4}$ inch on all four sides and mark this on the back of the matte.

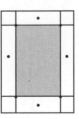

11. Tape the photo to the back of the matte so it is centered in the $\frac{1}{4}$-inch marks you just made. Turn the matte over and you are done.

Task

Using this Task

Students are to work in pairs on questions 1 and 2, writing and testing their instructions on matting a photo.

After this experience of writing and testing their instructions with a partner, each student should revise his/her directions and turn in his/her own finalized set.

Characterizing Performance

This section offers a characterization of student responses and provides indications of the ways in which the students were successful or unsuccessful in engaging with and completing the task. The descriptions are keyed to the *Core Elements of Performance.* Our global descriptions of student work range from "The student needs significant instruction" to "The student's work meets the essential demands of the task." Samples of student work that exemplify these descriptions of performance are included below, accompanied by commentary on central aspects of each student's response. These sample responses are *representative;* they may not mirror the global description of performance in all respects, being weaker in some and stronger in others.

The characterization of student responses for this task is based on these *Core Elements of Performance:*

1. Use visual reasoning, measurement, and calculations involving fractions to reason about rectangles in an applied setting.
2. Write a clear and complete set of directions.

Descriptions of Student Work

The student needs significant instruction.

The student does not show evidence of how to calculate the dimensions of the opening to be cut in the matte board, nor does the student assure that the opening is centered on the matte.

Student A

This student does not indicate any measurements that would be necessary to center and cut the opening from the matte board.

The student needs some instruction.

The student shows evidence of attempting to visually center the photograph and gives a reasonable set of directions using a visual method for centering and cutting an appropriate-size rectangle from the matte board. The student provides no measurements to assure that the photo is truly centered.

Student B

This student does not describe how to center the photograph. The student only suggests that the photo should be centered. Although once the photo is presumably centered, the student does describe how to create the overlap needed and thus an appropriate-size opening.

The student's work needs to be revised.

The student does some calculations to center the photo with an appropriate-size opening, but calculations are incomplete or instructions are difficult to follow.

Student C

Student C offers reasonable directions to successfully center the photo, but extra effort is required to follow the student's instructions. He includes the $\frac{1}{4}$-inch overlap, but is unclear in explaining exactly how this should be done. He also states that one should "cut the tracing out." It is unclear whether the student is referring to the original tracing (which centered the photo), or that which results *after* the overlap is included.

The student's work meets the essential demands of the task.

The student gives necessary measurements to assure a centered opening with the appropriate dimensions.

Student D

Although the directions in the task only ask students to describe how to cut the opening in the matte, this student offers the calculations that lead to the accurate measurements. The student's directions, "Now, measure the sides and outline with the answers you get" are vague, but her diagrams and measurements help the reader to successfully center the opening.

Student A

1. Measure From both sides of the paper to the center.

2. Then place the picture on the matt

3. After that, line the picture on the marks that you have made.

4. Figure how much room you need to have an extra piece of paper around the outer part of the border.

5. Now that you have the picture centered you can put everything together.

Directions
to framing a photograph

Step 1: Take photograph and matt and place in designated workspace.
Step 2: Center photograph in middle of matt board.

Step 3: Once picture is centered on matt, outline edges of picture with a marking pen.

Step 4: Remove picture from matt and set aside. Take a ruler and measure an 1/8 inch inward from just drawn line on all sides.

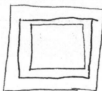

Step 5: Extend marks (1/8 inch marks) to solid lines which will form another square.
Step 6: Cut out most inner square
Step 7: Take picture and place underneath the matted opening (line up picture.)
Step 8: Use adheasive to attach picture to back of matt.

Student C

Rules:
1. Put the Photo in the lower left-hand corner.
then measure *from the top of the photo* to the top of the matte board
and divide that measurement by two.

2. Then measure to the right of the matte board
from the *Right side of the picture.*

3. *Take* the measurement from the top of the picture to
the top of the matte Board that you got ÷ 2. put
the picture that far down from the top of the
matte board. Do the same process for, the
side, Your picture is centered. Trace the
picture. Take it off. Inclose the tracing
by 1/4 of an inch. Cut the tracing out.
Put the picture on the other side of the
board. With a fourth of an inch of the
picture showing. Glue it on. Your done!

First measure your photo's legnth, and width
And the matte boards. Here is on example:

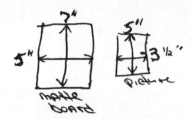

L: matte Board - pic = _____ ÷ 2 = _____ + 1/4 = _____

example =

L: 7 - 5 = 2 ÷ 2 = 1 + 1/4 = 1 1/4"

W: 5 - 3 1/2 = 1 1/2 ÷ 2 = 3/4 + 1/4 = 1"

Now, measure the sides and outline
with the answers you get =

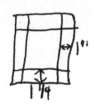

Cut out center And glue your picture
behind.

Reason using ratio and proportion.
Reason algebraically.
Generalize symbolically.

Grocery Store

Long Task

Task Description

This task asks students to consider the planning of a layout for a new grocery store. Students answer questions using scale models of shopping carts to solve problems related to the store's floor plan.

Assumed Mathematical Background

It is assumed that students have had experience with ratio and proportion and with generalizing linear situations symbolically.

Core Elements of Performance

- reason using ratio and proportion and successfully move back and forth between a real-world situation and a scale model to determine the lengths of shopping carts

- use algebraic reasoning to solve for an unknown and to generalize a linear relationship symbolically

- communicate mathematical reasoning

Circumstances

Grouping:	Students may discuss the task in pairs, but then complete an individual written response.
Materials:	rulers and calculators
Estimated time:	45 minutes

Grocery Store

This problem gives you the chance to

■ *reason about ratio and proportion*
■ *use algebraic reasoning*
■ *generalize symbolically*

Rasheed is planning the layout for a new grocery store. He found the diagram below in a supply catalog. It shows a drawing of a single shopping cart and a drawing of 12 shopping carts that are "nested" together. (The drawings are $\frac{1}{24}$th of the real size.)

length

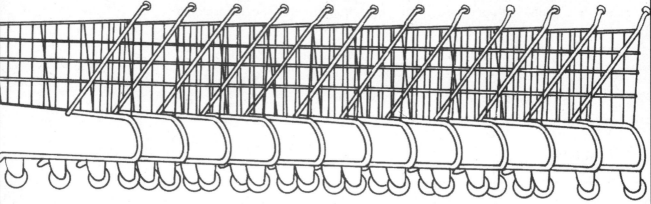

© *The Regents of the University of California*

Rasheed has several questions:

1. What is the length of a real shopping cart?

2. When the real carts are nested, how much does each cart stick out beyond the next one in the line?

3. What would be the total length of a row of 20 real nested carts?

4. What rule or formula could I use to find the length of a row of real nested carts for any (*n*) number of carts?

5. How many real nested carts could fit in a space 10 meters long?

Write a letter to Rasheed that answers his questions.

- For each question, explain your answer so that he can understand it and use it to make decisions about the store.

- To explain question 4, you may want to draw and label a diagram that tells what each part of your formula represents.

© The Regents of the University of California

Task

A Sample Solution

The following is a sample solution using centimeters. Students may also use inch measurements, although this will require conversion to metric for the last question.

Dear Rasheed,

Here are answers to your questions. I hope they will help you in planning your store. Good luck!

My answer to question 1—The length of a real shopping cart is **96 cm,** or .96 m. The scale model of a single shopping cart measures 4 cm. Since the scale is 1 to 24, multiply by 24 to get the real length: 4 cm × 24 = 96 cm.

My answer to question 2—Each cart sticks out beyond the next one in line approximately **26.4 cm** or about .26 m. In the scale model of the nested carts, I measured the distance between the handles on the first and second shopping carts and got about 1.1 cm (although it looks like it's a little more than that). You could measure in other ways too—by the grills, between the last two carts, and so on. Anyway, it comes out roughly the same. Then I multiplied by 24 to get the real length: 1.1 cm × 24 = 26.4 cm.

My answer to question 3—The total length of 20 nested carts is approximately **5.98 m.** In any row of nested carts, the first cart will take up 96 cm. Each additional cart will add 26.4 cm to the total length. Since you need the length of 20 carts, I added the length of one cart and 19 "stick outs" to get: 96 cm + (19 × 26.4 cm) = 597.6 cm or about 5.98 m.

My answer to question 4—If L is the total length in centimeters of n nested carts, then the total length of n nested carts is $L = 96 + 26.4(n - 1)$ which can be written as: $L = 26.4n + 69.6$. I got this formula in a way similar to finding the answer to your last question. The 96 is for the length of the first cart. After the first cart, there are $n - 1$ carts sticking out. So I multiplied the number of "stick outs" $(n - 1)$ by the length of each "stick out" (26.4) and added it all to the length of the first cart (96) giving me $L = 96 + 26.4(n - 1)$. Remember that this formula gives length in centimeters.

My answer to question 5—About **35 carts** could fit in a space 10 meters long. I got this answer by using the above formula and letting $L = 10$m. Since the formula finds length in centimeters, I let $L = 1000$ cm. Plugging in, I got $1000 = 26.4n + 69.6$. I solved for n: $n \approx 35.24$. Since you can't have parts of shopping carts, I rounded this number down to 35.

I hope that these answers help you to make decisions about your store.

Sincerely,
A. Student

Using this Task

Read the aims of the assessment in the box at the top of the first activity page. Read through the task. Students should be familiar with the context of this task. If not, have the class discuss how shopping carts are placed in a grocery store and what "nested" means. Students should work in pairs, but then hand in individual letters to Rasheed.

Issues for Classroom Use

This task places numerous demands on students. They must successfully move back and forth between the real world and scale model and use proportional reasoning, but they must also know when not to rely upon proportional reasoning alone. For example, students are often tempted to measure the 12 nested carts and use this information to answer question 3 (length of 20 nested carts) and question 5 (number of carts that fit in a 10 meter space) by reasoning proportionally. The results they obtain will be off but not by much. However, this type of reasoning shows a lack of attention to the first cart, which is a constant term—a central idea in linear functions, and an idea which students must account for in question 4 in order to produce a generalization that accurately represents the relationships in the situation.

Nevertheless, a purely proportional approach that ignores the constant term would not prove detrimental in the real world of shopping carts, especially when dealing with large numbers. As you increase the number of shopping carts, the relative effect of the greater length of the first cart (when compared to the stick-out length of each nested cart) decreases.

This task also involves issues of measurement. The questions do not indicate to students the level of accuracy required. Some students use rough measurements of the scale model while others strive for as much accuracy as possible. All reasonable responses are accepted.

Several questions related to accuracy could arise and you may want to discuss them with your class after students have completed the task. For example, how much should we rely on the accuracy of the scale model provided? What happens if we assume that it could be off by 5%? Is the 10 meter space a corral by the entrance of the store and is it fine if the carts stick out a bit? Or is the 10 meter space the width of a store room in which the carts must fit? How would Rasheed's purpose affect our answers? What other purposes might make us respond differently?

Task

Characterizing Performance

This section offers a characterization of student responses and provides indications of the ways in which the students were successful or unsuccessful in engaging with and completing the task. The descriptions are keyed to the *Core Elements of Performance.* Our global descriptions of student work range from "The student needs significant instruction" to "The student's work meets the essential demands of the task." Samples of student work that exemplify these descriptions of performance are included below, accompanied by commentary on central aspects of each student's response. These sample responses are *representative;* they may not mirror the global description of performance in all respects, being weaker in some and stronger in others.

The characterization of student responses for this task is based on these *Core Elements of Performance:*

1. Reason using ratio and proportion and successfully move back and forth between a real-world situation and a scale model to determine the lengths of shopping carts.
2. Use algebraic reasoning to solve for an unknown and to generalize a linear relationship symbolically.
3. Communicate mathematical reasoning.

Descriptions of Student Work

The student needs significant instruction.

Student may answer some questions correctly (either in the letter to Rasheed or beside the question), but does not successfully find an unknown (as in questions 3 and 5) or formulate a symbolic generalization (as in question 4).

Student A

Student A gives reasonable answers in questions 1 and 2 that show that she can measure and use information about scale, although it is unclear how she arrived at "26 centimeters" for question 2 ($1.2 \times 24 = 28.8$). For question 3, Student A seems to apply proportional reasoning to the 12 carts shown in the scale drawing. She appears to estimate that a drawing of 20 carts would measure 26.2 cm, but does not explain how she does this. For question 4, Student A's diagram shows attention to the first cart but she multiplies, rather than adding it to the n (actually $n-1$) carts and she does not include a length of each of the additional carts in her formula. In response to question 5, Student A says, "I cannot tell the answer very well." She guesses at an estimate but does not explain how she arrived at her guess.

The student needs some instruction.

Student successfully finds an unknown (questions 3 and 5), but does not demonstrate an understanding of how to arrive at a general formula.

Student B

Student B answers questions 1 and 2 correctly, although he does not explain to Rasheed how he found his answers. (We assume that he uses a measurement of 1 cm for the amount that each nested cart sticks out.) Student B also successfully answers questions 3 and 5. His estimate of 36 carts in question 5 is very well-reasoned and rather accurate relative to the measures he uses. However, Student B shows great difficulty in formulating a symbolic generalization of the situation. His verbal explanation of his formula (in the letter to Rasheed) shows how he reasoned through question 3, but instead of substituting $n-1$ for 19, he keeps 19 in his formula and then inserts n within it in various places. Student B does not use this formula for answering question 5 (it may not make sense to him), but instead reasons from the answer obtained in question 3.

The student's work needs to be revised.

Student successfully finds the unknown (questions 3 and 5) *AND* shows an understanding of how to generalize the situation, but fails to arrive at a completely correct formula.

Student C

Student C successfully completes many parts of the task but is inconsistent in a number of places. Her responses to questions 1 and 2 are correct, although given in different measurement units. Student C's explanations for questions 3 and 4 show solid reasoning about the situation and an understanding of how to generalize, but she confuses measures of the real and scaled world (1.1 comes from the scaled world and 96 from the real). This results in an incorrect formula as well as an unreasonable estimate for the length of 20 nested carts. In her response to question 5, Student C seems to abandon her estimate from question 3 and instead uses a more reasonable value of 16 feet without explaining how she arrived at this value.

Task

The student's work meets the essential demands of the task.

Student successfully finds the unknown and arrives at a correct generalization of the situation. Minor errors that do not distort the reasonableness of solutions are permitted.

Student D

Student D arrives at reasonable solutions to all questions. He communicates his reasoning well, only failing to state the measures he obtained from the scale model. His formula is complete and well-justified, as are his solutions to questions 3 and 5, although he mistakenly uses 900 cm as an equivalent value to 10 meters.

Rasheed has several questions:

1. What is the length of a real shopping cart? The length of a real shopping cart would be about 96 centimeters long. 24*4(cm)=96 24 is the size of the scale 4 is how long the sm. carts are.

2. When the real carts are nested, how much does each cart

   stick out beyond the next one in the line? On the diagram carts they stick out about 1.2 centemeters in the real cart size the carts would stick out about 26 centemeters. (1.2*24=.50÷10=2 1*24+2 =26)

3. What would be the total length of a row of 20 real nested

   carts? a total row of 20 carts in the sm diagram would be about 26.2 cm long. a total row of 20 real carts would be about 626. 24*26.2 =626

4. What rule or formula could I use to find the length of a row

   of real nested carts for any (*n*) number of carts?
   L= 4N*24 (If you use the diagram on the previous page.)

5. How many real nested carts could fit in a space 10-meters

   long? About 2 to3 nested carts could fit in a 1 meter space. So in a 10 meter space about 20 to 30 could fit.

Write a letter to Rasheed that answers his questions.

■ For each question, explain your answer so that he can

   understand it and use it to make decisions about the store.

■ To explain question 4, you may want to draw and label a

   diagram that tells what each part of your formula represents.

Dear Rasheed,

For the first question you asked concerning the shopping cart problem you would take the diagram and measure it in cm. then multiply it by 24 (because diagram is 1/24th of the real model) For the final answer I get 96 cm.

In the second question you would measure the space each shopping cart sticks out from one another. Then you would multiply that by 24 (because the diagram is 1/24 of the real thing). For the final answer to that problem I get 26 cm.

For the third question you would measure the length of the shopping carts nested in the small diagram in cm. Then you would multiply it by 24, your answer after you multiply would be the total size in which the real carts are.

In the fourth question you asked what the total length would be when the row of nested carts is 'n'. For that question I would take

(4 * N) * 24 and that would give you a total answer for a unknown number of real nested carts. (Look at diagram below on 1st sheet)

For the fifth question I can not tell the answer very well, but my guess for it is about 20 to 30 carts could fit in a 10 meter space. When and/or if you find the answer to #5 write me back and tell me it please.

4's diagram

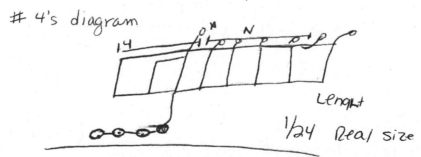

1. 4 cm * 24 = 96 cm
2. They Are sticking 24 cm from the next over in line
3. 19·24 = 456 + 96 = 552
4. L = 96 + 24 n · 19 n = 552
5. If 20 carts is 552 cm And there is 100 cm in. in A meter than 20 carts is about 5 meters long, so 40 carts is 1104, but that is A little over 10 meters but if you take four carts away you will be just under 10 meters so I think the Answer is 38 carts in 10 meters

Dear Rasheed,

I hope my answers will be sygnifigant to you.
The length of A shopping cart is 96 cm long. When the carts
Are nested together each cart sticks out 24 cm from the
one in front of it. The equation to figure out the length
of "n" nested carts is L = 96 n + 24 n • 19 n = 552. to make this
You take the length of the first cart 96 cm then each
carts sticks out 24 cm And there is 19 of them so you
times 24 by 19 And the Answer plus 96 cm then there is your
Answer

You can use this to Answer question 5 wich is 36.

1. The length of an individual, real size shopping cart is 96 centimeters

2. When the carts are nested together each cart sticks out 12 inches beyond the next cart in line.

3. The length of all 20 nested carts should be 116.9 cm

4. $L = (n-1)1.1 + 96$

5. If you have a space that is 10 meters long you could fit into that space 40 carts.

Mr. Rasheed,

    I am writing this letter to inform you of your questions concerning the grocery store shopping carts. Since the length of the diagram shopping cart is 1:24 you multiply the length of the diagram cart, which comes out to be 4cm. by 24 and get 96cm for a life size cart. When the carts are nested together in the diagram they stick out a half an inch from the next one. To make this real you would again multiply the .5 inch by 24 to come up with 12 inches. If you have 20 carts you take the 1st cart out and take the other 19 and multiply them by 1.1 because that is the distance that each cart sticks out from the next one. Then you add on the 1st cart which is 96cm to come up with a length of 116.9 cm. To find the length of "n" nested carts you take the "n" and subtract one. Then multiply that by 1.1 and add 96. Refer to diagram at the end of letter. If you had a space that was 10 meters long and you wanted to know how many carts could fit in that space you can say that there are about 3 feet in a meter and with a 10 meter space that would be 30 feet The length of 20 nested carts is about 16 feet, which is a little over half of thirty, so there would be about 40 carts in a 10 meter space

$$n - 1 \cdot \boxed{Cart} + 96$$
$$\underbrace{}_{1.1}$$

Dear Rasheed,

The real length of a shopping cart is 96cm. We found this multipling the scale drawing by 24 because the drawing is 1/24 of a real shopping cart. When the carts are nested together each cart sticks out 24 centimeters. We found this the same way we found the length of a real length of a shopping cart. The total length of a row of 20 nested carts is 552 centimeters We found this by taking 96cm. for the first cart then multiplying 24cm for the amount each cart sticks out by 19 for the rest of the carts. To find the total length for "n" nested carts use the equation $T = 96 + 24(n-1)$ In the equation the "T" stands for the total length, the 96 stands for the first cart, the 24 stands for the amount each cart sticks out, and the "n" stands for the number of nested carts. About 34 carts nested together would take up about 10 meters. We found this by subtracting 96 cm for the first cart from 900cm (10 meters) leaving us with 804 cm., then we divide that by 24 for how much the cart sticks out and that leaves us with about 33 carts plus the first one that equals 34 carts.

Locate points and
determine slope.

Find angle measure
and area.

Name perpendicular
and parallel lines.

Pentagon

Long Task

Task Description

Students are given a pentagon drawn on a Cartesian plane. They find the
coordinates of points, estimate the measures of angles, determine which
line segments are parallel and perpendicular, and find slope and area.

Assumed Mathematical Background

It is assumed that students have had some experience with finding points
on the Cartesian plane, estimating angles, and determining slope and area.

Core Elements of Performance

- use knowledge of Cartesian plane to locate points and determine
  slopes
- reason geometrically to estimate angles, name perpendicular and
  parallel line segments, and calculate area

Circumstances

Grouping:	Students complete an individual written response.
Materials:	No special materials are needed for this task.
Estimated time:	40 minutes

Pentagon

This problem gives you the chance to

■ *locate points, determine slopes, estimate angle measures, and calculate area*

Pentagon ABCDE is shown below.

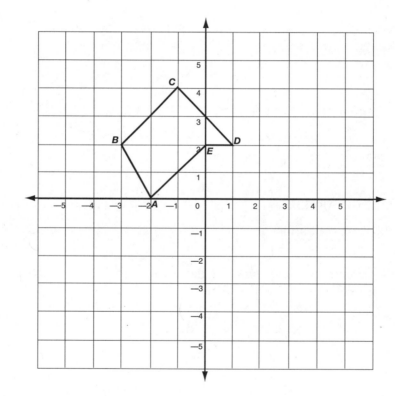

1. What are the coordinates of the following points?

   a. B is at _____

   b. C is at _____

2. Estimate the measures of the following angles *inside* the pentagon.

   a. Angle AED is about _____

   b. Angle ABC is about _____

   c. Explain how you determined your answer to 2a.

© The Regents of the University of California

3. a. List pairs of sides of pentagon ABCDE that are **parallel,** if any.

   b. Explain how you determined your answer to 3a.

4. a. List pairs of sides of the pentagon that are **perpendicular,** if any.

   b. Explain how you determined your answer to 4a.

5. Give the slope of each of the following line segments.

   a. slope of $\overline{AB}$ is _____   **b.** slope of $\overline{BC}$ is _____

   c. Explain how you determined your answer to 5a.

6. a. What is the area of pentagon ABCDE?

   b. Explain how you determined your answer to 6a.

© The Regents of the University of California

Task **A Sample Solution**

1a. B (–3, 2)

1b. C (–1, 4)

2a. Angle AED is about 225°.

2b. Angle ABC is about 108°.

2c. Angle AED is the sum of a 180° angle and a 45° angle. A straight line has 180° and line segment $\overline{AE}$ appears to bisect one of the squares on the grid. Therefore angle AEB is 45°. Reasonable estimates of angle AED range from 215° to 235°.

Angle DBA (part of angle ABC) appears to be about $\frac{2}{3}$ of one of the right angles at B. Therefore, 60° + 45° (for angle DBC) equals 105°, a good estimate for angle ABC. Reasonable estimates of angle ABC range from 95° to 115°.

Angle ABC is about 108° because it is the sum of a 45° angle and approximately a 63.4° angle. It appears $\overline{BC}$ bisects a 90° angle resulting in the 45° angle. Using the grid and the Pythagorean theorem results in line segment $\overline{AB}$ having a length of $\sqrt{5}$. The arccos of $\left(\frac{1}{\sqrt{5}}\right) \approx 63.43°$.

More on the Mathematics

3a. Line segment $\overline{AE}$ is parallel to $\overline{BC}$.

3b. They both have the same slope, 1. If you extend the line segment, they will always be the same distance apart. They never meet.

4a. $\overline{BC}$ is perpendicular to $\overline{CD}$.

4b. Their slopes are the negative reciprocals of each other. $\overline{BC}$ has a slope of 1 and $\overline{CD}$ has a slope of –1. Also, since both $\overline{BC}$ and $\overline{CD}$ bisect grid squares that each form 45° angles with the grid line, their sum is 90° and therefore they are perpendicular.

5a. The slope of $\overline{AB}$ is –2.

5b. The slope of $\overline{BC}$ is 1.

5c. Slope is the change in the *y*-units per change in *x*-units. The slope of segment $\overline{AB}$ is $\frac{+2}{-1} = -2$ and the slope of segment $\overline{BC}$ is $\frac{+2}{+2} = 1$.

6a. The area of pentagon ABCDE is 7 square units.

6b. Solution A: Inside pentagon ABCDE there are 3 complete square units and 6 half squares. Also, line segment $\overline{AB}$ bisects 2 square units, adding one more square unit: $3 + 6(\frac{1}{2}) + 1 = 7$.

Solution B: Draw a 4-by-4-unit square with corners at (1, 0), (1, 4), (–3, 4), and (–3, 0) around pentagon ABCDE. The total number of square units is 16. Outside of the pentagon there are 9 square units— 5 whole squares, 6 half squares and one more square (from the two squares bisected by line segment $\overline{AB}$). Therefore, pentagon ABCDE has an area of 16 square units – 9 square units = 7 square units.

Task

Characterizing Performance

This section offers a characterization of student responses and provides indications of the ways in which the students were successful or unsuccessful in engaging with and completing the task. The descriptions are keyed to the *Core Elements of Performance*. Our global descriptions of student work range from "The student needs significant instruction" to "The student's work meets the essential demands of the task." Samples of student work that exemplify these descriptions of performance are included below, accompanied by commentary on central aspects of each student's response. These sample responses are *representative;* they may not mirror the global description of performance in all respects, being weaker in some and stronger in others.

The characterization of student responses for this task is based on these *Core Elements of Performance:*

1. Use knowledge of Cartesian plane to locate points and determine slopes.
2. Reason geometrically to estimate angles, name perpendicular and parallel line segments, and calculate area.

Descriptions of Student Work

The student needs significant instruction.

Student may give a few correct answers about coordinates, angle measures, parallel lines, perpendicular lines, slope, or area but provides little, if any, mathematical justification for those correct answers.

Student A

Student A gives correct answers for questions 1, 3a, and 4a but her justification for the latter two is simply based on how the figure looked. She seems to lack fundamental knowledge about slope that would give her the tools to answer and justify her answers to several of the questions. She demonstrates some reasoning about her answers to question 2, but her estimates of the size of some angles is not close. Her answer to question 6a is not even a close estimate and her explanation does not make sense.

The student needs some instruction.

Student gives correct answers to some but not all questions reflecting a lack of understanding about some key ideas (for example, the student may demonstrate knowledge of angle measurement but not about slope). Student provides mathematical justifications for some but not all correct answers and justifications may be weak.

Student B

Student B gives correct answers to questions 1, 3a, 5a, 5b, and 6a. The explanations for questions 3b and 5c are weak but provide some evidence of understanding of slope. The incorrect answers for question 2 and no answer for question 4 suggest a lack of understanding about angle measures.

The student's work needs to be revised.

Student answers nearly all questions correctly and provides strong mathematical justifications for some of the answers indicating knowledge of most of the key ideas (coordinates, angle measures, parallel and perpendicular lines, slope, and area). Some explanations are weak.

Student C

Student C gives correct answers to all questions except number 6 (gives an estimate of the perimeter rather than area). He claims in question 4b that "they form a 90° angle" without making an argument, but his reasoning in question 2c suggests that he has reasonable ways of determining angles on the grid. In his explanation for 3b, he does not provide an argument for how he knows that the two lines are the same distance apart.

The student's work meets the essential demands of the task.

Student answers all questions correctly and gives a strong explanation for most of the answers.

Student D

Student D responds correctly to all of the questions and uses angle measures to determine parallel and perpendicular lines. The student's explanation for finding slope is a bit weak since slope is referred to as going to the right and going up. On the other hand, Student D has calculated the slopes correctly for lines with a negative and a positive slope, respectively.

Pentagon ABCDE is shown below.

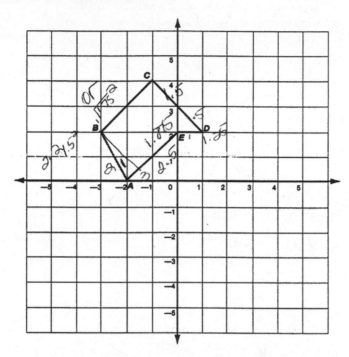

1. What are the coordinates of the following points?
   a. B is at (-3,2)   b. C is at (-1,4)

2. Estimate the measures of the following angles *inside* the pentagon.
   a. Angle AED is about 150°   b. Angle ABC is about 140°
   c. Explain how you determined your answer to 2a.

Woops this is the outside

I looked at at and Saw that there was a 90°∠ and it looked like 60 added to it. 60+90=150. I estimated the one side to be about 60° and the other to be about 60° w/20° added to it. 60+60+20=140°.

3. a. List pairs of sides of pentagon ABCDE that are **parallel**, if any.

$(\overline{B,C} + \overline{AE})$

b. Explain how you determined your answer to 3a. I looked at the picture and saw that they will parallel

4. a. List pairs of sides of the pentagon that are **perpendicular**, if any. $\overline{B,C}$, $\overline{D,C}$

b. Explain how you determined your answer to 4a.

I looked at the diagram.

5. Give the slope of each of the following line segments.

a. slope of $\overline{AB}$ is ___, ___   **b.** slope of $\overline{BC}$ is _____

c. Explain how you determined your answer to 5a.

6. a. What is the area of pentagon ABCDE?

$\simeq 4.125$

b. Explain how you determined your answer to 6a.

I found the perimeter + lengths and then cut the pentagon into 2 triangles & a rect., then I added them together.

Pentagon

This problem gives you the chance to

■ *locate points, determine slopes, estimate angle measures, and calculate area*

Pentagon ABCDE is shown below.

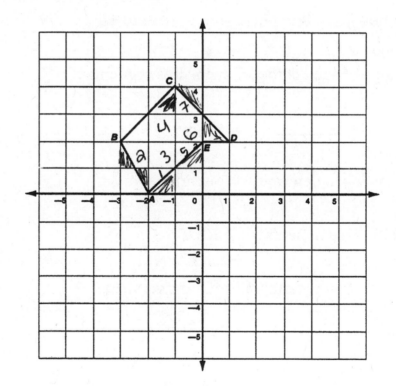

1. What are the coordinates of the following points?

   a. B is at (-3,2)   **b.** C is at (-1,4)

2. Estimate the measures of the following angles *inside* the pentagon.

   a. Angle AED is about 120   **b.** Angle ABC is about 60

   c. Explain how you determined your answer to 2a.

   I guessed by what they looked like

3. a. List pairs of sides of pentagon ABCDE that are **parallel**, if any.

$$\overline{BC} \parallel \overline{AE}$$

b. Explain how you determined your answer to 3a.

They are about the same length at the same angle with the same distance apart.

4. a. List pairs of sides of the pentagon that are **perpendicular**, if any.

b. Explain how you determined your answer to 4a.

I don't think there are any.

5. Give the slope of each of the following line segments.

a. slope of $\overline{AB}$ is ___-2___   **b.** slope of $\overline{BC}$ is ___1___

c. Explain how you determined your answer to 5a.

Just looked to see how much the points moved by

6. a. What is the area of pentagon ABCDE?

7 units

b. Explain how you determined your answer to 6a.

I counted the squares

Pentagon

This problem gives you the chance to

■ *locate points, determine slopes, estimate angle measures, and calculate area*

Pentagon ABCDE is shown below.

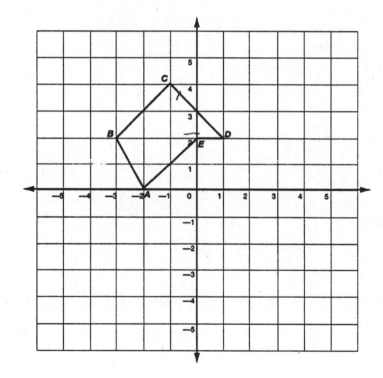

1. What are the coordinates of the following points?

   a. B is at ‾3,2   **b.** C is at ‾1,4

2. Estimate the measures of the following angles *inside* the pentagon.

   a. Angle AED is about 275°   **b.** Angle ABC is about 100°

   c. Explain how you determined your answer to 2a.
   on i it looks like a 180° I guessed on it & a 45° angle out together

3. **a.** List pairs of sides of pentagon ABCDE that are **parallel**, if any.

$\overline{AE} - \overline{BC}$

   b. Explain how you determined your answer to 3a.

On $\overline{AE}$ it is the same distance from anywhere on the line to $\overline{BC}$

4. **a.** List pairs of sides of the pentagon that are **perpendicular**, if any.

$\overline{BC} - \overline{DC}$

   b. Explain how you determined your answer to 4a.

They form a 90° angle

5. Give the slope of each of the following line segments.

   a. slope of $\overline{AB}$ is ____ -2 ____   **b.** slope of $\overline{BC}$ is ____ 1 ____

   c. Explain how you determined your answer to 5a.

i) for every one it goes over, it goes down two
ii) for every 1 it goes over, it goes up 1

6. **a.** What is the area of pentagon ABCDE?

9

   b. Explain how you determined your answer to 6a.

it is 9 units around

Pentagon

This problem gives you the chance to

■ *locate points, determine slopes, estimate angle measures, and calculate area*

Pentagon ABCDE is shown below.

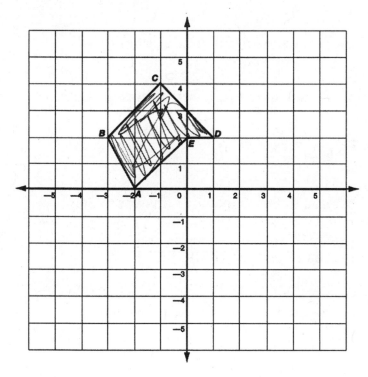

1. What are the coordinates of the following points?

   a. B is at $(-3, 2)$ **b.** C is at $(-1, 4)$

2. Estimate the measures of the following angles *inside* the pentagon.

   a. Angle AED is about $225°$ **b.** Angle ABC is about $113°$

   c. Explain how you determined your answer to 2a.
   The line from E (on the graph) made a 90° angle. AE made a 45° angle so I added them together: 360 - 135 = 225.

3. a. List pairs of _sides_ of pentagon ABCDE that are **parallel,** if any.

$\overline{BC} + \overline{AE}$

b. Explain how you determined your answer to 3a.

They both form A 45° Angle.

4. a. List pairs of sides of the pentagon that are **perpendicular,** if any. $\overline{CD} + \overline{CB}$

b. Explain how you determined your answer to 4a.
∠C is 90°, CD + CB divide A 90° Angle in half 90÷2=45

5. Give the slope of each of the following line segments.

a. slope of $\overline{AB}$ is ___-2___   **b.** slope of $\overline{BC}$ is ___1___

c. Explain how you determined your answer to 5a.
For every unit you go to the right, however in : Any units up is the slope.

6. a. What is the area of pentagon ABCDE?

7 units

b. Explain how you determined your answer to 6a.

Counted squares.

half A box + half box = 1 box

⅓ A box + ⅔ a box = 1 box

Reason about probability.

Justify a decision.

Communicate mathematical reasoning.

Lucky Draw

Long Task

Task Description

Students use theoretical and/or experimental probability to determine the profitability of a festival game. They write a report to the festival committee explaining their recommendation.

Assumed Mathematical Background

It is assumed that students have had experience with finding theoretical and experimental probability.

Core Elements of Performance

- analyze and reason about probability to determine the profitability of a carnival game
- make and justify a recommendation to an audience

Circumstances

Grouping:	Following a class introduction, students complete an individual written response.
Materials:	red and blue colored counters or cubes, 3 large cups (for class demonstration), and additional cups for students
Estimated time:	40 minutes

Lucky Draw

This problem gives you the chance to

- *analyze and reason about probability*
- *make and justify a decision*
- *communicate mathematical reasoning*

At the Palatine School's fall festival, the Charity for Children Club is planning to run a money-raising booth. One of the members in the club proposed the following game:

Lucky Draw

Win $1.00

10¢ per turn

There are equal numbers of red and blue balls buried in sawdust in each barrel.

One turn allows you to make
ONE LUCKY DRAW from each barrel for 10¢.
If you draw three balls of the same color on one turn you win $1.00.

Elida, the chairperson of the festival, likes the idea of the game, but she wants to make sure it is a good money maker. As co-chairperson, you have been asked to prepare a report to the festival committee on this issue. Make sure that your report includes your recommendation and clearly explains how you came to your conclusion.

© The Regents of the University of California

A Sample Solution

Theoretical Approach A

I believe that this game is not a good fund raiser. I figured out the following about the game:

- An equal number of red balls and blue balls means that there is a $\frac{1}{2}$ probability of drawing either red or blue from each barrel.

- If I want to draw three red balls (one from each barrel), then the probabilities must be multiplied: $\frac{1}{2} \times \frac{1}{2} \times \frac{1}{2}$. This is the same for three blue balls.

- So the probability of getting three balls of the same color is $\frac{1}{8}$ for red and $\frac{1}{8}$ for blue. So, together there is a $\frac{1}{4}$ probability of winning the $1.00 prize.

- That means that for every four players, one of them should win. The game would take in $0.40 for every four players and pay out $1.00, leaving the charity $0.60 behind. So they could expect to lose $0.60 ÷ 4 players or $0.15 per player on average when a lot of people play this game.

If a lot of people were to play this game, a lot of money could be lost and there would be no profit at all. I would not recommend this game to Elida as a "money maker."

Theoretical Approach B

To find out if the game would be profitable, I made a tree diagram. *R* is a red ball. *B* is a blue ball.

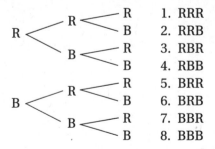

The diagram shows that there are eight different ways of drawing red and blue balls from the three barrels. Two of them, RRR and BBB, give the player a win. So there is a $\frac{2}{8}$ or $\frac{1}{4}$ chance of winning. So for every eight plays, the charity would take in $0.80 and pay out $2.00, which gives them a loss of

Task

$1.20. If a lot of people played this game, they would lose a lot of money. The game needs to be changed.

Experimental Approach

I played this game by putting an equal number of red and blue chips in three cups and then drew a chip from each cup 50 times (without looking). I put the chips back in their cups and mixed the chips very well after each play. Here are my results for the game:

Losses

37 losses
Charity club makes $3.70
(Each player paid $0.10,
so 37 × $0.10 = $3.70.)

Wins

13 wins
Charity club pays $11.70
(Each player paid $0.10, but the charity
club paid out $1.00 to each of them,
so 13 × $1.00 = $13.00 – $1.30 = $11.70.)

Overall in this game, experimental probability shows that for every 50 players, we would make $3.70 on the losses and pay out $11.70 on the wins, giving a total loss of $8.00. I think I played this game enough times to show what will happen when a lot of people play it. I would expect that the charity will lose a lot of money with this game. It needs to be changed.

Using this Task

For Formal Assessment

Hand out the task to students and read the aims of the assessment in the box at the top of the activity page. Read through the task with students and make sure they understand the context of the task. You may want to model the game with colored cubes or counters and cups. Have such materials available for students to use while completing the task. Answer any questions about the *context* of the task, but if students ask what form of probability they should use (experimental or theoretical), tell them it is their choice.

Issues for Classroom Use

Students may choose to use either theoretical or experimental probability to determine whether or not the game is profitable. If students use only experimental probability, a complete response must include an explanation of how the game was modeled (for example a student could draw three times from only one cup, replacing each ball after each draw) and must involve a large number of trials (50 or more). If students use *both* theoretical and experimental probability, a high-level response would include some discussion about the differences in the findings, the meanings of the two findings, and a reconciliation between the two in the recommendations to the festival committee.

This task may be extended in numerous ways. If many students use experimental probability, have them share the different findings and discuss why they may differ from each other and from the theoretical findings. Pose or have students pose different questions or change the parameters of the game (for example, what if there were four barrels to draw from, or *n* barrels? What if there were three different colors of balls? What if there were twice as many red balls as blue balls? What if we didn't know whether there were equal numbers of each color ball in each barrel?). Alternately, have students play with the different parameters—including cost to play and cost of prize—and have them design a profitable game.

Task

Characterizing Performance

This section offers a characterization of student responses and provides indications of the ways in which the students were successful or unsuccessful in engaging with and completing the task. The descriptions are keyed to the *Core Elements of Performance*. Our global descriptions of student work range from "The student needs significant instruction" to "The student's work meets the essential demands of the task." Samples of student work that exemplify these descriptions of performance are included below, accompanied by commentary on central aspects of each student's response. These sample responses are *representative*; they may not mirror the global description of performance in all respects, being weaker in some and stronger in others.

The characterization of student responses for this task is based on these *Core Elements of Performance:*

1. Analyze and reason about probability to determine the profitability of a carnival game.
2. Make and justify a recommendation to an audience.

Descriptions of Student Work

The student needs significant instruction.

Student shows some attempt at reasoning through the task, but does not show understanding of how to apply probability analysis to the situation.

Student A

Student A shows some attempt at reasoning through the task. He recommends charging a higher price (60¢) to play the game and correctly determines that with a 10¢ cost to play, "they would lose lots of moolah." His diagram (with the Bs and Gs) may represent some attempt at modeling the theoretical probability of winning the game, but his reasoning is unclear.

The student needs some instruction.

Student uses probability to reason through the task, but the student's reasoning is based only on experimental probability with an insufficient number of trials (less than 50) *OR* student does not model theoretical outcomes completely and correctly.

Student B

Student B correctly determines that the game is not profitable based on her experimental findings, but she conducts only 15 trials, an insufficient number. Student B also models the game incorrectly. Although she placed equal amounts of red and blue balls in a bowl and closed her eyes, she appears to have drawn all three balls at once, without replacing them in between draws. This would have affected the probabilities of the different possible outcomes.

Student C

Student C's tree diagram correctly lists all of the possible theoretical outcomes. However, Student C does not base his reasoning on this model. He explains, "It's a one in ten chance [of winning], so they wouldn't make very much money." Student C's theoretical probability model indicates a one in four chance of winning. He seems to base his reasoning on his experimental findings, shown in his diagram. This being the case, he conducted too few trials (only 10).

The student's work needs to be revised.

Student correctly determines that the game is not profitable through correct use of either theoretical or experimental probability, but student does not produce a clear and complete report directed to the festival committee.

Student D

Student D correctly uses theoretical probability to model the possible outcomes, to determine the probability of winning the game: "p (all r or b) = $\frac{2}{8}$," and to determine that the game would lose money (actually he shows how a player would make money). However, Student D does not direct his comments to the festival committee. He first says that the game is not fair (perhaps thinking that in a fair game, players have an equally likely chance to win or lose). Then as if talking to a player, he explains how you have a pretty good chance of winning money. (Student D also makes an arithmetical error. He says, "You would make 50¢." He should say, "60¢.")

Task

The student's work meets the essential demands of the task.

Student correctly uses experimental and/or theoretical probability to determine profitability and recommends rejecting the game *AND* student writes a clear and complete report to the festival committee, justifying the decision. (This includes an explanation of a correct modeling of the game if experimental probability is used.)

Student E

Student E correctly uses theoretical probability to determine the chances of winning the game and the profitability of the game. She writes a clear report to the committee, including sufficient justification of her recommendation. In addition, so that the game can produce a profit, Student E recommends a change in the cost to play and she explains the theoretical profit for the revised game.

Student A

Recommendation

I think that they should charge
60¢ for each game , because its'
too easy to win right now
and if they charged 10¢ they would
lose lots of moolah

< 2 B-6
   C -6
   B- B

Lucky Draw

Yes ▨▨▨   NO ▨▨▨

| | | | = 4 $ ЖНТ ЖНТ | | = 00 = 150

No it is not a good money-maker because
you loose 2.50 on the winnings the
Customer gets. The Customer would
have only spent 1.50 on 15 games
and the workers would have to give
back the Customer's money plus
2.50 more because that
Customer won. I got my conclusion
by putting 4 red balls and 4 blue
balls into a bowl and I closed my
eyes and picked out 3 balls.

Experimental:

Same	different
I	⊔⊔ IIII

Theoretical

P ⟨ P ⟨ P
           G
     G ⟨ P
           G

G ⟨ P ⟨ P
           G
     G ⟨ P
           G

Possible outcomes:

P-P-P
P-P-G
P-G-P
P-G-G
G-P-P
G-P-G
G-G-P
G-G-G

No, I don't think it's a good money maker because as soon as they get a dollar, someone wins so they don't get any money. It's a one in ten chance, so they wouldn't make very much money.

(rrr)   (bbb) $P\left(\begin{array}{c}\text{All r or}\\ \text{b}\end{array}\right) = 2/8$

rrb   bbr $P\left(\begin{array}{c}\text{not all}\\ \text{r or b}\end{array}\right) = 6/8$

rbr   brb

rbb   brr

It's not fair because you have a 1/4 chance of winning. You have a 3/4 chance of not winning. You have a pretty good chance of winning because theoreticaly if you draw 4 times then you'll win 1 time. If you, play 4 times thats only 40¢ to play, You would win 1 dollar ou would make 50¢.

Student E

Notes, Resarch

Barrel #1	Barrel #2	Barrel #3
10¢ →R	R	R
10¢ →R	R	B
10¢ →R	B	R
10¢ →R	B	B
10¢ →B	B	B
10¢ →B	B	R
10¢ →B	R	B
10¢ →B	R	R

Out of eight draws you'd be expected to win twice. But if you only play once and win the booth will lose money.

Because in 8 turns you make 80¢ and lose $2.00, a lose At $1.20

Report

Elida is right, how it's set up now you probley wouldn't make any or much money. My reccomendation is to charge anywhere from 30¢ to 45¢ a turn. Because if you charge 35¢ and the person draws 8 times theoreticly, you would make $2.80. If the person won twice, you would lose $2.00, profits theoreticly for 8 turns is only 80¢. To come to this conclusion I first made an orginized list of all the possibilities. There were 8. Each person payed 10¢, 8 times 80¢, and winning twice is 2.00, 2.00 lose $1.20, not good therefore raise your price or lessen your prize.

Describe the location of a
design on a grid.

Brian's
T-shirt

Long Task

Task Description

This task asks students to describe a geometric design for a T-shirt (that
combines arcs and several segments on a grid) to a friend over the phone so
that he can reproduce the design.

Assumed Mathematical Background

It is assumed that students have had experience with systems for locating
points, lines, shapes, and circles on a grid. Students may use nonconventional and invented systems to locate the design.

Core Elements of Performance

- locate the placement of all parts of a design (semicircles, line
  segments) on a grid

- use an efficient and systematic approach (may be an invented
  system)

- give a clear set of directions

Circumstances

Grouping:	Students complete an individual written response.
Materials:	No special materials are needed for this task.
Estimated time:	30 minutes

Brian's T-shirt

This problem gives you the chance to

- *systematically communicate about geometric shapes*
- *locate shapes on a grid*
- *give a clear set of directions*

The design below, including the 8-by-10 grid, is going to be used on a math team T-shirt. You accidentally took the original design home, and your friend, Brian, needs it tonight. Brian has no fax machine, but he does have an 8-by-10 grid just like yours. (See Brian's grid on the next page.) You must call Brian on the telephone and tell him very precisely how to draw this design on his grid.

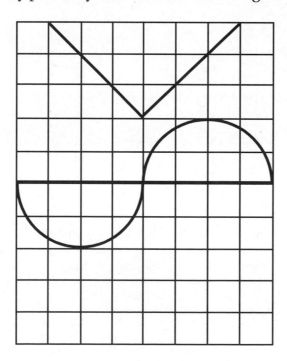

© The Regents of the University of California

On Your Own

This is the grid that Brian has in front of him. Prepare for your phone call by writing out your directions. Once you have finished, check your work to make sure that Brian will be able to recreate the design from your description.

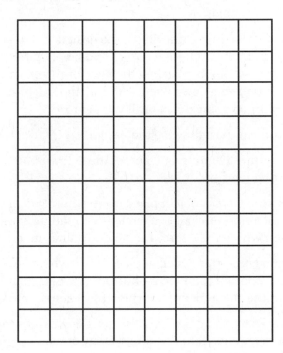

© The Regents of the University of California

Task

A Sample Solution

The following are three alternative sample solutions.

A. This solution uses an invented coordinate system similar to the Cartesian coordinate system.

Before you begin the drawing of the design you need to label the 8-by-10 grid. Start in the upper-left corner and label that first dark line "1." Then going across, number each of the lines until you get to 9. Now, do the same thing going down. Start with the upper-left dark line and label that "1." Continue going down until you get to 11.

Now you can start drawing the design.

1. First draw a line straight across the 6 down line from left to right, cutting your grid in half.

2. Keeping your pencil in place (from where you ended in step 1), draw a semicircle—**top** half of a circle—with radius 2 units and a center at the point where the 7 across and 6 down lines meet.

3. Again keep your pencil in place (from where you ended in step 2) and draw another semicircle—**bottom** half of a circle—with radius 2 units and a center at the point where the 3 across and 6 down lines meet.

4. Now go to where the 5 across and 4 down lines meet. You will draw two line segments from this point. Draw one line segment from this point to where the 8 across and 1 down lines meet. Draw another line segment from this point to where the 2 across and 1 down lines meet.

5. The finished picture should look like the letter *V* above two semicircles.

B. The Cartesian coordinate (*x, y*) system is another system that students may use to describe the design.

Number the vertical lines from left to right along the bottom of your grid from 0 to 8. This is your *x*-axis. Then number the horizontal lines from bottom to top along the left side of your grid from 0 to 10. This is your *y*-axis. I will specify points on the grid by giving the *x*-value first and then the *y*-value.

Now you can start drawing the design.

1. Draw a straight line across the grid from (0, 5) to (8, 5).

2. Keeping your pencil in place, draw the upper half of a semicircle with radius 2 units and a center point at (6, 5).

3. Keeping your pencil in place from step 2, start at (4, 5) and draw the lower half of a semicircle with radius 2 units and a center point at (2, 5).

4. Starting at point (4, 7), draw a line segment to point (7, 10). Draw another line segment from (4, 7) to (1, 10).

5. The finished picture should look like the letter *V* above two semicircles.

C. Another system students may use involves numbering the boxes of the grid from 1 to 80.

Begin by numbering the boxes across starting with 1 from the upper-left corner. Once you have reached 8 and filled the first row of boxes, start the next row by numbering across left to right, from 9 to 16. Continue in this manner until you have filled all the boxes and reached 80.

With the boxes thus numbered, directions can be given that are similar to those given in solutions A and B. Each point may be specified by naming the four boxes that share a common corner (and one number for boxes on the perimeter). For example, to make the *V* shape, draw a line from the upper-left corner of the box numbered 2 to the corner shared by boxes numbered 20, 21, 28, and 29. Next, draw a line from that same corner to the upper-right corner of the box numbered 7. The directions for drawing the semicircles should be given in the same manner.

Task **Using this Task**

For Formal Assessment

Distribute this task to students and read the following or paraphrase it closely.

Who is wearing a T-shirt today? [Identify students who are wearing a T-shirt with a design, picture, or words printed on their shirt.] Does anyone know how this is done? [It is a prepared design which is heat-transferred onto the shirt, or perhaps silk-screened.]

This activity is about someone who has designed a T-shirt logo and needs to describe it to someone over the phone.

Would someone please read the directions? [You may want to ask other students to clarify the directions, but do not discuss how to do the task.] Would someone read the aims of the assessment in the box at the top of the page?

Since you have to write directions in this problem, you will be communicating mathematically. Think about how well your friend can understand your directions. In fact, when you are finished, you can read your directions to yourself as though you were your friend on the other end of the phone. Ask yourself, "Would I know what to draw from the directions?" Think about how accurately Brian would draw the picture from the directions you have given. Will everything in the design be in Brian's picture? Will the design be in the right place on the grid?

Think about how you could check your directions after you are finished. One thing you could do to try checking your work would be to use the blank grid included with the task to try drawing the design *from your directions*.

Issues for Classroom Use

This task does not require students to use the conventional Cartesian coordinate system. Students may use nonconventional and invented systems as well as conventional coordinate ones for locating the design.

Characterizing Performance

This section offers a characterization of student responses and provides indications of the ways in which the students were successful or unsuccessful in engaging with and completing the task. The descriptions are keyed to the *Core Elements of Performance.* Our global descriptions of student work range from "The student needs significant instruction" to "The student's work meets the essential demands of the task." Samples of student work that exemplify these descriptions of performance are included below, accompanied by commentary on central aspects of each student's response. These sample responses are *representative;* they may not mirror the global description of performance in all respects, being weaker in some and stronger in others.

The characterization of student responses for this task is based on these *Core Elements of Performance:*

1. Locate the placement of all parts of the design (semicircles, line segments) on a grid.
2. Use an efficient and systematic approach (may be an invented system).
3. Give a clear set of directions.

Descriptions of Student Work

The student needs significant instruction.

Student uses no system for locating parts of the design and makes major errors in placement or distorts the shape of the design.

Student A

Student A does not use a system and gives inaccurate directions that could invariably lead to great distortions of the design. For example, the direction, "on the left side of that line make a half circle 4 × 2 so that it looks like a spoon" requires a great deal of guessing on the part of a reader (hearer) to decide what to do.

Task

7

The student needs some instruction.

Student attempts a system for locating all parts of the design but the system does not have the potential for locating points precisely. This results in errors in placement or a lack of relationship between the whole design and its parts *OR* considerable effort is needed to follow the directions.

Student B

Student B attempts a system, but does not explain how to number her grid. At times she gives numbers as if they identify boxes and at other times she mentions lines. This could cause distortions in placement of parts of the design as well as an upside-down design.

The student's work needs to be revised.

Student gives a system that addresses all parts of the design, which has the potential for locating points precisely, but the system is inefficient, resulting in inaccuracies. Some effort may be needed to follow the directions.

Student C

Student C addresses all parts of the design, most of which with a great deal of accuracy. Although the system is not the most efficient, Student C compensates by being very precise. However, there is a potential for distortion of some of the design; Student C is not clear about exactly where to place the two semicircles.

Student D

Student D uses a coordinate system for locating some parts of the design, although it is executed with some imprecision. It is unclear exactly how to connect the dots in step 2, and where to place the "4 unit circles" in step 3. Furthermore, Student D does not state whether "4 units" in the circles refers to their radius, diameter, or circumference.

The student's work meets the essential demands of the task.

Student gives a complete, efficient system that is capable of locating all parts of the design with reasonable accuracy *AND* directions that are clearly stated and easy to follow.

Student E

Student E gives a complete and efficient system and locates all parts of the design, although there are a few potential places for distortion or confusion. Student E does not state whether to begin from the top or bottom when labeling lines A–K. Incorrect labeling could cause an upside-down design. In the last sentence of the directions, Student E says "top" instead of "bottom." However, these places for confusion are minor and it is quite likely that a reader (hearer) would accurately reproduce the design from these directions.

Student A

On Your Own

This is the grid that Brian has in front of him. Prepare for your phone call by writing out your directions. Once you have finished, check your work to make sure that Brian will be able to recreate the design from your description.

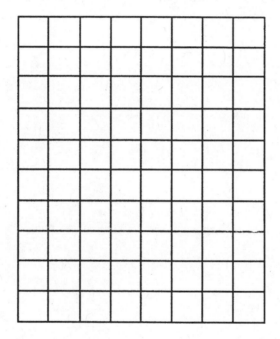

Going from side to side make
a line in the middle. on the
left side of that line make
a half circle 4x2 so it looks
like a spoon. Then do the same
thing on the right but on the
top of the line instead of the
bottom. Then from the second square at
the top makein up side down triangle down 3 squares
and up 3 squares diaganaly.

What you need to do is at the top left corner of your grid go over 1square. You need to be in the left corner of that square. Then from there you go to the bottom right hand corner. Then you go from the left corner to the right where you ended up at. Then from there from the left corner to the right corner again. Now you should be three down and four over. Then from that corner go to the right hand corner so you should end up at the right top corner 3 down and 5 over. Then from there keep going diagonal till you end up in the top right hand corner on the first line 7 over. Then you need to go 5 down and in between square 5+6, make a straight line across. You then need to make a dot 7 down, 2 over. Another dot on 5 down, 5 over. You need 1 more dot on 4 down, 6 over. You then connect the dots with half circles that would be those sizes.

Turn your paper so that the 10 squares are up & down

• Now go in 1 square on the left and on the right

• go to the top left corner of the 2nd square on the left & put a dot there

• Now go to the top right corner of the 2nd square on the right and put a dot.

• Now go back to the left side of the paper. go down 3 squares and then over 4. Put a dot in the lower right corner of the 4th square.

• Now from the dot you just made, draw a straight diagonal line to the top left of the same square.

• From that, draw a straight, diagonal line through all centers of the rest of the squares up to the dot you made before on the left.

• Now do the same thing out to the right side. You should have a triangle

• Next go down 5 squares and draw a straight line all the way across. It should split that rectangal in ½ now

• On the right side above the line — make a ½ circle with a diameter of 4 & a radius of 2

• On the left side under the line — make a ½ circle with a diameter of 4 & a radius of 2

0. Make a graph. In left hand corner put 0 and go up and over by 1's.

1. Draw a dark horizontal line through the middle starting the 5 on the y axis.

2. Play conect the dots. Put a dot at (1,10) then (4,7) then (7,10) make sure you connected the dots

3. Use the line you made in step 1 and draw two 4 unit circles. There sould be just enough room. Don't let them over lap.

4. Erase the top <u>half</u> of the circle on the left so it looks like a bowl

5. Erase the bottom half of the right circle so it looks like a upsiddown bowl. Then you are done.

Student E

Label the top of the grid 0-8 on the lines. On the left of it label them A-K on the lines. On 1,A to 4-D Draw a line then To T-A From 4-D. The draw a line across F. Then on F-4 to F-8 draw a rainbow shape. The top should touch between 5.5, D to 6.5, D. Then do the same thing on the bottom except on 0-F to 4F. The top should touch on 1.5. H to 2.5, H to get another rainbow shape.

Find and compare areas. Use visual and/or numerical reasoning.

Grass for Goats

Short Task

Task Description

Students are given the context of a goat grazing in a yard. Students determine the area of grass that the goat can reach when it is kept on a chain that is 3 meters long.

Assumed Mathematical Background

It is assumed that students have had experience finding the areas of circular regions.

Core Elements of Performance

- use visual, geometric, and/or numerical reasoning to find circular regions
- compute and compare areas

Circumstances

Grouping:	Students complete an individual written response.
Materials:	compass and ruler
Estimated time:	20 minutes

Grass for Goats

This problem gives you the chance to

- *use visual, geometric, and numerical reasoning*
- *calculate and compare areas*

The Jacobsens keep their goat on a chain that is 3 meters long.

1. If they chain the goat to a metal hook in the center of their yard, what is the area of the grass that the goat can reach to eat? Sketch a picture and show your work.

2. Sometimes the Jacobsens chain the goat to the corner of a shed that is 5 meters by 4 meters. The 3-meter chain is

© The Regents of the University of California

attached to the base of the wall at ground level. What is the area of grass that the goat can reach? Show and explain your work.

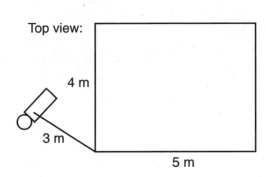

Top view:

4 m

3 m

5 m

3. Suppose the goat was chained at ground level to the center of the 4-meter shed wall. Would the amount of grass the goat can reach be greater than what he could reach when chained to the corner of the shed? Justify your answer.

© The Regents of the University of California

Task **A Sample Solution**

1. The goat can reach 3 meters in any direction. Therefore, the goat can reach a circular area of radius 3 meters.

   Area = $\pi \times 3^2 = 9\pi \approx 28.27$ square meters

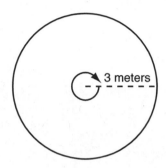

2. The goat can still reach 3 meters in any direction except for the area covered by the corner of the shed. The corner of the shed makes a 90-degree angle so the shed covers the area of one-fourth of the original circle. Therefore, the goat can reach an area three-fourths of a circle of radius 3 meters.

   Area = $\frac{3}{4}(\pi \times 3^2) \approx 21.21$ square meters

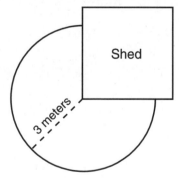

3. This question asks the student to compare two areas. It can be answered either by computing the second area and comparing numerical values or by making visual/geometric comparisons.

   The goat can reach a semicircular area in front of the shed and he can reach around the shed on both sides as shown in the following picture.

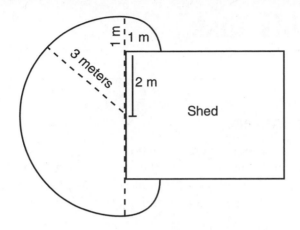

A computational response

The semicircular region is half of a circle of radius 3 meters: Area = $\frac{1}{2}$ ($\pi \times 3^2$) ≈ 14.14 square meters. Since the shed's corners are right angles, the two additional regions on the sides of the shed are each a quarter of a circle of radius 1 meter. Taken together, they are one half of a circle of radius 1 meter: Area = $\frac{1}{2}$ ($\pi \times 1^2$) ≈ 1.57 square meters. Add these two areas to get the total area, which is approximately 15.71 square meters.

The amount of grass the goat can reach when chained to the center of the shed wall is less than when chained to the corner since 15.71 square meters is *less* than 21.21 square meters.

A visual response

When the goat is chained to the corner of the shed, he can reach the area in Figure 1 below. When he is chained to the center of the shed, he can reach the area in Figure 2 below. The semicircles A and C have the same area. If you superimpose regions D and E on B, you can see in Figure 3 that they do not cover B. So the area the goat reaches in Figure 2 (chained to middle of the shed) is less than in Figure 1 (chained to the corner).

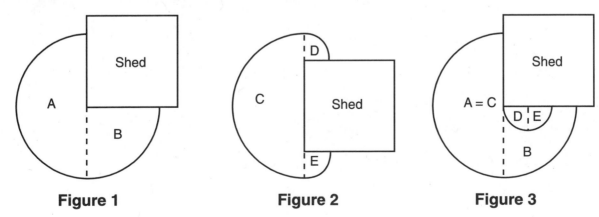

Figure 1   **Figure 2**   **Figure 3**

Task

Using this Task

For Formal Assessment

Review the aims of the assessment in the box at the top of the first activity page. Read the problem aloud to your students. Because this task is short and straightforward, it would be appropriate to simply hand out the task and leave students to read and answer the questions individually.

Issues for Classroom Use

Some students may raise the issue that the chain is around the goat's neck and therefore the goat's mouth can reach just beyond 3 meters. Other students may calculate areas using a length less than 3 meters since the chain reaches from the ground up to the goat's neck. (Although when the goat is eating, his neck is very close to the ground.) Both interpretations are acceptable so long as the students maintain these perspectives throughout the task.

Characterizing Performance

This section offers a characterization of student responses and provides indications of the ways in which the students were successful or unsuccessful in engaging with and completing the task. The descriptions are keyed to the *Core Elements of Performance*. Our global descriptions of student work range from "The student needs significant instruction" to "The student's work meets the essential demands of the task." Samples of student work that exemplify these descriptions of performance are included below, accompanied by commentary on central aspects of each student's response. These sample responses are *representative*; they may not mirror the global description of performance in all respects, being weaker in some and stronger in others.

The characterization of student responses for this task is based on these *Core Elements of Performance:*

1. Use visual, geometric, and/or numerical reasoning to find circular regions.
2. Compute and compare areas.

Descriptions of Student Work

The student needs significant instruction.

Student engages in the task, but shows serious errors in finding the areas of circles.

Student A

Student A shows no evidence of being able to find the area of a circle. In his response to question 1, he seems to remember that a measurement of circles involves squaring the radius. He answers "9" and states this as the value of the circle's circumference. In response to question 2, Student A shows that he remembers 360° is somehow related to circles, but this information cannot help in answering the question. For question 3, Student A correctly determines that the goat can reach less grass when chained to the center of the shed than when chained to the corner. However, he incorrectly reasons that the goat can only reach half a circle when chained to the center.

Task

8

The student needs some instruction.

Student correctly computes the area of the circle in question 1 but makes significant errors in visual, geometric, and/or numerical reasoning in response to question 2 and/or question 3 *OR* student demonstrates some correct reasoning about area but not enough to make this measure.

Student B

Student B uses the formula for circumference rather than for area all the way through the task. This is a significant error. Her reasoning on questions 2 and 3 would have yielded correct results had she used a correct formula. For example in question 3, Student B finds what she believes is the total area of grass for the goat by taking half her area for a 3-meter circle and adding half of her area for 1-meter circle; her values are incorrect.

The student's work needs to be revised.

Student correctly determines and computes the areas of the regions in questions 1 and 2. In question 3, student correctly states that the goat can reach less grass when chained to the center of the shed, but reasoning and/or justification is incomplete or incorrect.

Student C

Student C gives correct responses to questions 1 and 2 (he apparently used 3.14 as the value for π). He does not, however, fully explain his response to question 2. He correctly responds "no" to question 3, but his reasoning is incorrect since he does not account for the areas the goat can reach on both sides of the shed.

The student's work meets the essential demands of the task.

Student correctly determines and computes the areas of the regions in questions 1 and 2, correctly compares areas in question 3, and provides reasonable justification.

Student D

Student D gives correct numerical values and reasonable explanations in response to questions 1 and 2. In question 3, the student correctly computes the area of grass the goat can reach when chained to the center of the shed. Student D draws a thorough sketch and explains his computations, although he never directly states which situation allows the goat to reach a greater area of grass.

The Jacobsens keep their goat on a chain that is 3 meters long.

1. If they chain the goat to a metal hook in the center of their yard, what is the area of the grass that the goat can reach to eat? Sketch a picture and show your work. a circle with the circumference of 9 meters

2. Sometimes the Jacobsens chain the goat to the corner of a shed that is 5 meters by 4 meters. The 3-meter chain is attached to the base of the wall at ground level. What is the area of grass that the goat can reach? Show and explain your work.

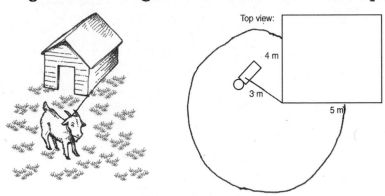

Top view:

4 m

3 m

5 m

120 meters because you take 360°
because it makes a circle and divide it
by 3 how many meters you have and
you get 120.

3. Suppose the goat was chained at ground level to the center of the 4-meter shed wall. Would the amount of grass the goat can reach be greater than what he could reach when chained to the corner of the shed? Justify your answer.

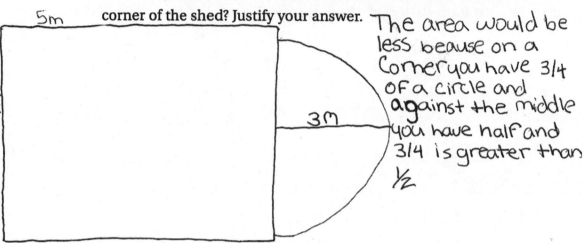

The area would be less beause on a Corner you have 3/4 of a circle and against the middle you have half and 3/4 is greater than ½

Student B

The Jacobsens keep their goat on a chain that is 3 meters long.

1. If they chain the goat to a metal hook in the center of their yard, what is the area of the grass that the goat can reach to eat? Sketch a picture and show your work.

$$A = 2\pi r$$
$$A = \pi 6$$
$$6 \cdot \pi \approx 18.849$$
$$A \approx 18.849^2 \text{ meters}$$

2. Sometimes the Jacobsens chain the goat to the corner of a shed that is 5 meters by 4 meters. The 3-meter chain is attached to the base of the wall at ground level. What is the area of grass that the goat can reach? Show and explain your work.

Top view:

4 m

3 m

5 m

I got the Area there would be if there was not a shed. I divided the Area into 4 quarters. The shed takes up 1 quarter, so I times it by 3

$$A = 2\pi r$$
$$A = \pi 6$$
$$6 \cdot \pi \approx 18.849$$
$$18.849 \div 4 = 4.71225$$
$$4.71225 \cdot 3 = 14.13675$$
$$A \approx 14.13675$$

3. Suppose the goat was chained at ground level to the center of the 4-meter shed wall. Would the amount of grass the goat can reach be greater than what he could reach when chained to the corner of the shed? Justify your answer.

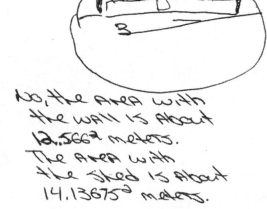

No, the Area with the wall is about 12.566² meters.
The Area with the shed is about 14.13675² meters.

$A = 6\pi$
$18.849 \div 4 = 4.71225$
$4.71225 \cdot 2 = 9.4245$

$A = 2\pi$
$6.283 \div 4 = 1.57075$
$1.57075 \cdot 2 = 3.1415$
$9.4245 + 3.1415 = 12.560$

Student C

The Jacobsens keep their goat on a chain that is 3 meters long.

1. If they chain the goat to a metal hook in the center of their yard, what is the area of the grass that the goat can reach to eat? Sketch a picture and show your work.

The goat can reach 28.26 sq meters of grass.

Radius sq - 9 × Pi = 28.26

2. Sometimes the Jacobsens chain the goat to the corner of a shed that is 5 meters by 4 meters. The 3-meter chain is attached to the base of the wall at ground level. What is the area of grass that the goat can reach? Show and explain your work.

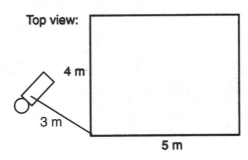

Top view:

4 m

3 m

5 m

The goat can reach 21.2 sq. meters of grass.

7.06 cannot reach

$$28.26$$
$$-\ 7.06$$
$$\overline{21.2}$$

3. Suppose the goat was chained at ground level to the center of the 4-meter shed wall. Would the amount of grass the goat can reach be greater than what he could reach when chained to the corner of the shed? Justify your answer.

No, because this amount —>

is only 2/3 of this amount —>

The Jacobsens keep their goat on a chain that is 3 meters long.

1. If they chain the goat to a metal hook in the center of their yard, what is the area of the grass that the goat can reach to eat? Sketch a picture and show your work.

$A = \pi R^2$ $A = \pi \cdot 3^2 = 28.27 \ M^2$

R = 3M.

First I recalled that the area of a circle equals $\pi \cdot R^2$ the radius is 3 meters. $\pi \cdot 3^2$ would give me the area. Since it it are the answer would be 28.27 M^2.

28.274333887 whole number area

2. Sometimes the Jacobsens chain the goat to the corner of a shed that is 5 meters by 4 meters. The 3-meter chain is attached to the base of the wall at ground level. What is the area of grass that the goat can reach? Show and explain your work.

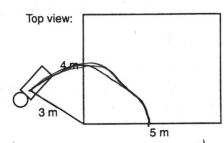

Top view:

4 m

3 m

5 m

$A = 21.205$

$A = \pi r^2$

$R = 3$

$\pi \times 3^2/4 = 28.27433388$

$7.0685 \ 83471 \times 3 =$

$21.205 \ 75041$

First I took the whole number from the previous question and divided it by four to see how big each section or quarter of the circle would be. Then I multiplied it by three to find out the area of three sections and leave out the corner of three sections and leave out corner of the shed. Or you can multiply the area times 3/4 to find out the area also which is quicker.

3. Suppose the goat was chained at ground level to the center of the 4-meter shed wall. Would the amount of grass the goat can reach be greater than what he could reach when chained to the corner of the shed? Justify your answer.

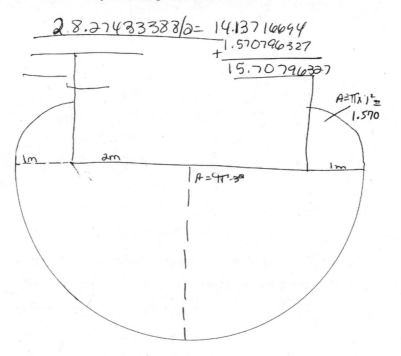

First I took the whole number from the last questions and divided it by two for the area of a half circle and then took the area of 4 divided by two and added them together to make 15.707

9

Picnic

Read, interpret, and compare decimals.

Operate with rational numbers.

Short Task

Task Description

Students are given a grocery store advertisement that lists various specials. They use the data to determine the cost per student to hold a picnic.

Assumed Mathematical Background

It is assumed that students have had experience operating with rational numbers.

Core Elements of Performance

- read, interpret, and compare decimals
- operate with rational numbers

Circumstances

Grouping:	Students complete an individual written response.
Materials:	No special materials are needed for this task.
Estimated time:	20 minutes

Picnic

THURSDAY FOOD SECTION
PICNIC SEASON AT FOODALL!

Cola 12-Pack $3.20   **Cola 6-Pack $1.60**

Cola 24-Pack $4.24

Watermelon!!!
(Weight: approx. 7 pounds each)
First of the season . . . $5.50 each!

Hamburger Meat:
$1.49 per pound!
(Limit: 5 pounds per customer.
Additional: $1.79 per pound)

Hamburger Buns
$0.39 per package of 8

© The Regents of the University of California

Picnic

> **This problem gives you the chance to**
> - *work with decimals to find the best price for an item*
> - *use decimals, fractions, and percents to solve problems*

Mr. Miller's sixth-grade class is planning an end-of-year picnic. They use the given grocery store advertisement to help them make their plans. Chris and Luis agree to buy the food, if everyone shares the cost. In addition to sharing the cost of the food, Mr. Miller says he will bring the ketchup, mustard, napkins, paper plates, and cooking supplies.

Chris wants to see which cola packaging is the cheapest. Using the advertisement she writes:

The 6-pack is $1.60.

The 12-pack is two 6-packs, so I divide $3.20 by 2 on the calculator.

The 24-pack is four 6-packs, so I divide $4.24 by 4 on the calculator.

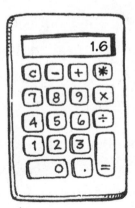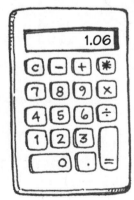

© The Regents of the University of California

1. Chris says, "The six pack costs $1.60. The calculator indicates that the 12-pack costs 1.6 per 6-pack and the 24-pack costs 1.06 per 6-pack. I'm not sure which is the cheapest."

   Write a short note to Chris explaining how the three cola packages compare. Tell Chris which is the best buy and explain why.

PICNIC MENU
✓ Hamburger on a bun
✓ Watermelon
✓ Can of soda

2. Mr. Miller says, "Plan on a quarter pound of hamburger per person." Luis says, "One seven-pound watermelon will serve 12 to 15 people." Chris says, "There are 21 people in the class, including Mr. Miller and us."

© The Regents of the University of California

How much money should Chris and Luis collect for food from each student (including themselves) and Mr. Miller? Use the food advertisement and show all your work.

3. Chris's mom finds a coupon for 5% off a grocery bill from Foodall. If Chris and Luis use this coupon, how much will they now need to collect from each person for the picnic. Explain how you found your answer.

© The Regents of the University of California

Task **A Sample Solution**

9

1. Chris,
   The 24-pack is the best buy since the price per 6-pack is lowest. The 12-pack and 6-pack each cost $1.60 per 6 cans while the 24-pack costs $1.06 per 6 cans. When the calculator shows "1.6," that means $1.60.

2. Cost of hamburger:
   (0.25 lb per person)(21 people) = 5.25 lbs
   [5 lbs at $1.49 per lb = $7.45] + [0.25 lbs × $1.79 per lb = $0.4475, or $0.45] = $7.90

   Cost of buns:
   Buns cost $0.39 for a package of 8. Three packages will be needed for 21 people ($0.39 per package)(3 packages) = $1.17.

   Cost of watermelon:
   If one watermelon serves 12 to 15 people, then two watermelons are enough for 21 people. (2 watermelons)($5.50 per watermelon) = $11.00

   Cost of soda:
   We'll buy a 24-pack since it's the best buy. One 24-pack costs $4.24.

   Total cost of the food is $7.90 + $1.17 + $11 + $4.24 = $24.31.

   $24.31 ÷ 21 people = $1.157619 per person. This number needs to be rounded to $1.16 per person, so we have enough money.

3. **Method 1:** Our savings is 5% of $24.31 = $1.2155 (which needs to be rounded to $1.22). Our new total cost of food is $24.31 − $1.22 = $23.09. The new cost per person is $23.09 ÷ 21 people ≈ $1.10 per person (again, rounded to the nearest whole cent). *OR*, we can calculate the discount per person: 5% of $1.16 per person = $0.058 ≈ $0.06. The discounted cost per person is $1.16 − $0.06 ≈ $1.10.

   Method 2: A coupon of 5% means we only have to pay 95% of original bill. ($24.31)(0.95) = $23.09 total, $23.09 ÷ 21 people ≈ $1.10 per person. *OR*, the cost per person is 95% of original cost per person: ($1.16 per person)(0.95) ≈ $1.10 per person.

   Some students may suggest collecting an "easier" amount of money, for example, $1.20 instead of $1.16. The use of the extra money could be discussed.

Using this Task

For Formal Assessment

After handing out the task to the students, review the aims of the assessment in the box at the top of the activity page. Because this task is short and straightforward, it would be appropriate to simply hand out the task and leave students to read and answer the questions individually.

Issues for Classroom Use

Some areas charge tax on food or beverages or charge a deposit on cans. If this is true in your community these additional costs may change how students respond to the task questions. It is appropriate for students to account for these costs in their solutions.

Task **Characterizing Performance**

9

This section offers a characterization of student responses and provides indications of the ways in which the students were successful or unsuccessful in engaging with and completing the task. The descriptions are keyed to the *Core Elements of Performance*. Our global descriptions of student work range from "The student needs significant instruction" to "The student's work meets the essential demands of the task." Samples of student work that exemplify these descriptions of performance are included below, accompanied by commentary on central aspects of each student's response. These sample responses are *representative*; they may not mirror the global description of performance in all respects, being weaker in some and stronger in others.

The characterization of student responses for this task is based on these *Core Elements of Performance:*
1. Read, interpret, and compare decimals.
2. Operate with rational numbers.

Descriptions of Student Work

The student needs significant instruction.

Student engages in the task but demonstrates little understanding of rational numbers and does not address the task.

Student A

Student A correctly chooses the 24-pack as the best buy and he explains why. He does some computations, however, that seem unrelated to the task, for example, "3 gos into 12, 4 times." His cost per student is not reasonable and his discounted cost per student is incorrect and not relative to his cost per student.

The student needs some instruction.

The student demonstrates some understanding of rational numbers. The student accurately performs minor calculations or correctly interprets Chris's soda cost calculations *BUT* he/she does not give enough work to address the task.

Student B

Student B states that the 24-pack is the best buy, but her explanation that "1.06 is the amount more a 24 pack is than a 6 pack" is incorrect. She does not include the cola and buns when determining the total cost of the picnic. Moreover, Student B does not calculate the cost of the hamburger at two different rates. She does not determine the discounted rate per student and her discounted total is not relative to her total cost.

The student's work needs to be revised.

Student demonstrates knowledge of rational numbers by answering most questions correctly and by providing some clear and complete explanations.

Student C

Student C explains that the 24-pack is the best buy. She correctly calculates the cost of the watermelons, buns, and soda. However, Student C's cost of hamburger, $52.45, is not reasonable. This number is so far off that it shows lack of reasoning. Her discounted cost is relative to her total cost, but she does not figure out the discounted cost per student.

The student's work meets the essential demands of the task.

Student demonstrates knowledge of rational numbers by answering all questions correctly and providing clear and complete explanations.

Student D

Student D explains that the 24-pack is the best buy. He correctly finds the cost of each of the picnic items and includes the different rates per pound of hamburger. Student D correctly calculates the original and discounted cost per student.

Student A

1. Chris says, "The six pack costs $1.60. The calculator indicates that the 12-pack costs 1.6 per 6-pack and the 24-pack costs 1.06 per 6-pack. I'm not sure which is the cheapest."

   Write a short note to Chris explaining how the three cola packages compare. Tell Chris which is the best buy and explain why. If you buy ~~the~~ four 6 packs & a 6 pack cost 1.6 that = $6.40. If you buy a 24-pack that = 4 packs & the cost is $4.24. Each pack cost 1.06 & you save 54¢ on each pack.

   PICNIC MENU
   ✓ Hamburger on a bun
   ✓ Watermelon
   ✓ Can of soda

2. Mr. Miller says, "Plan on a quarter pound of hamburger per person." Luis says, "One seven-pound watermelon will serve 12 to 15 people." Chris says, "There are 21 people in the class, including Mr. Miller and us."

Student A

How much money should Chris and Luis collect for food
from each student (including themselves) and Mr. Miller?
Use the food advertisement and show all your work.

I took 3 gos into 15, 5 times. 3 gos into 12, 4 times
if you add three that is 50 that = 4/5. 5.50 ÷ 5 = 1.1
1.1 × 4 = 4.4, 12 + 12 = 24 so each kid has 12
little left over. 5.5 + 5.5 = 11 so each kid
pays 53¢.

3. Chris's mom finds a coupon for 5% off a grocery bill from
Foodall. If Chris and Luis use this coupon, how much will
they now need to collect from each person for the picnic.
Explain how you found your answer. 42¢ the 5% off
every dollar so I ÷ 11 ÷ 5 = 2 11 − 2.2 = 8.8.
.42 × 21 kids = 8.82.

1. Chris says, "The six pack costs $1.60. The calculator indicates that the 12-pack costs 1.6 per 6-pack and the 24-pack costs 1.06 per 6-pack. I'm not sure which is the cheapest."

Write a short note to Chris explaining how the three cola packages compare. Tell Chris which is the best buy and explain why.

1.06 would be the cheapest because that is a 24 pack. 1.06 is the amount More a 24 pack is then a 6 pack.

PICNIC MENU

✓ Hamburger on a bun
✓ Watermelon
✓ Can of soda

2. Mr. Miller says, "Plan on a quarter pound of hamburger per person." Luis says, "One seven-pound watermelon will serve 12 to 15 people." Chris says, "There are 21 people in the class, including Mr. Miller and us."

How much money should Chris and Luis collect for food from each student (including themselves) and Mr. Miller? Use the food advertisement and show all your work.

$1.49 \div 4 = .3725$
$.3725 \times 21 = \$7.82$
Hamburger

$5.50 \div 2 = 2.75$
$15 \div 2 = 7.5$
$15 + 7.5 = 22.5$
Watermelon

5.50
$+2.75$
8.25

Each person = \$1.30
$21 \div 16.07$

\$16.07
Total

3. Chris's mom finds a coupon for 5% off a grocery bill from Foodall. If Chris and Luis use this coupon, how much will they now need to collect from each person for the picnic. Explain how you found your answer.

$21 \div$

Total
\$11.07

1. Chris says, "The six pack costs $1.60. The calculator indicates that the 12-pack costs 1.6 per 6-pack and the 24-pack costs 1.06 per 6-pack. I'm not sure which is the cheapest."

   Write a short note to Chris explaining how the three cola packages compare. Tell Chris which is the best buy and explain why.

   A six pack costs 1.60 two six packs cost 3.20 (or a 12 pack) A 24 pack is 4,6 packs so it should cost 6.40 or 1.60 per 6 pack but it only costs 4.24 or 1.06

   ## PICNIC MENU
   ✓ Hamburger on a bun
   ✓ Watermelon
   ✓ Can of soda

2. Mr. Miller says, "Plan on a quarter pound of hamburger per person." Luis says, "One seven-pound watermelon will serve 12 to 15 people." Chris says, "There are 21 people in the class, including Mr. Miller and us."

How much money should Chris and Luis collect for food
from each student (including themselves) and Mr. Miller?
Use the food advertisement and show all your work.

Its better to have left overs
than shortage so,,,2 water melons
5,25 pounds everybody bring
in 328

watermelon 11.00

meat 52.45
     4.24
buns 1.17   Total 68.86÷21=3.274047619   so,,,about 3.28

3. Chris's mom finds a coupon for 5% off a grocery bill from
   Foodall. If Chris and Luis use this coupon, how much will
   they now need to collect from each person for the picnic.
   Explain how you found your answer.

68.86 - 5% 65.42

1. Chris says, "The six pack costs $1.60. The calculator indicates that the 12-pack costs 1.6 per 6-pack and the 24-pack costs 1.06 per 6-pack. I'm not sure which is the cheapest."

   Write a short note to Chris explaining how the three cola packages compare. Tell Chris which is the best buy and explain why.

   The 12 pack is 1.6 dollars or $1.60 per 6 can. The same as the price of the 6 pack. The 24 pack costs 1.06 dollars on $1.06 per 6 cans so it is the cheapest because $1.06 per 6 pack is less than $1.60 per 6 pack. So the 24 pack is the cheapest.

   ## PICNIC MENU
   ✓ Hamburger on a bun
   ✓ Watermelon
   ✓ Can of soda

2. Mr. Miller says, "Plan on a quarter pound of hamburger per person." Luis says, "One seven-pound watermelon will serve 12 to 15 people." Chris says, "There are 21 people in the class, including Mr. Miller and us."

How much money should Chris and Luis collect for food
from each student (including themselves) and Mr. Miller?
Use the food advertisement and show all your work.

$2 \times 5.50 = \$11.00$ watermelon

$21 \times .25 = 5.25$ lbs hAmburger

$5.00 \times 1.49 = \$7.45$ $\$7.90$

$.25 \times 1.79 = \$0.45$

Pop $= \$4.24$

$11.00 + 7.90 + 4.24 + 1.17 =$
$\rightarrow 24.31$

Buns $= 3 \times .39 = \$1.17$

They should collect 1.16 or $24.31 \div 21 = 1.1576$
To make it easier $\$1.25$

3. Chris's mom finds a coupon for 5% off a grocery bill from
   Foodall. If Chris and Luis use this coupon, how much will
   they now need to collect from each person for the picnic.
   Explain how you found your answer.

1.10 I took 5% off of $24.31 \times \div$ it
by $21.$

10

Polygon Measures

Find angle measures, perimeters, and areas of regular polygons.

Reason about relationships between regular polygons.

Short Task

Task Description

Students are given a regular nonagon and a regular decagon of equal length sides drawn on grid paper. They are to find angle measure, perimeter, and area for the nonagon. They are asked to compare and explain the angle measures of the decagon in relation to the nonagon.

Assumed Mathematical Background

It is assumed that students have had experience with geometric shapes and their properties.

Core Elements of Performance

- find angle measures, perimeters, and areas
- reason and compare visually and geometrically about measures of two regular polygons

Circumstances

Grouping:	Students complete an individual written response.
Materials:	angle rulers or protractors
Estimated time:	20 minutes

Polygon Measures

This problem gives you the chance to

- *find angle measurements*
- *find perimeter and area of figures*
- *compare regular polygons*

Designers are experimenting with new tile shapes for walls and floors.

- The tile here is in the shape of a regular *nonagon.*
- The regular *nonagon* has nine equal sides and angles.

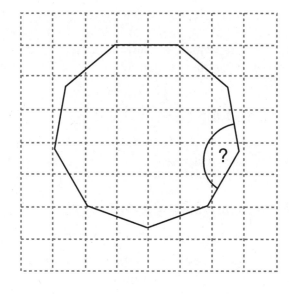

1. What is the measure of the angle marked in the figure? _____ (Use any measuring tool that will help you.)

2. Estimate the area of the nonagon. _____ Explain how you got this answer.

3. Estimate the perimeter of the nonagon. _____ Explain how you got this answer.

4. Will nonagons make good ceramic tiles for floors and walls? Use the geometric properties of the nonagon to explain or illustrate why or why not.

© *The Regents of the University of California*

Designers have developed another tile shape.

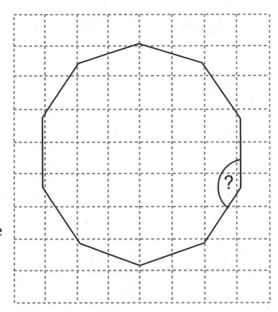

- The tile here is in the shape of a regular *decagon*.

- A regular decagon has ten equal sides and angles.

- The sides of this decagon are the same length as those of the nonagon.

5. Without using any measuring tools, decide whether the angle marked in this decagon is larger or smaller than the angle marked in the nonagon. Explain why this is so.

6. Is the perimeter of the decagon greater, smaller, or the same as the nonagon? Explain how you know.

7. Is the area of the decagon greater, smaller, or the same as the nonagon on the previous page? Explain your reasoning.

© The Regents of the University of California

Task **A Sample Solution**

1. 140°

2. 23 square units or 24 square units (square centimeters) are both reasonable answers. There are 18 whole squares and 8 partial squares, each at least one-half of a whole square, totaling at least 4 whole squares. Estimate the remaining 4 partial squares to total 1 whole square, 18 + 4 + 1 = 23.

3. 18 units. A side in the top of the drawing was 2 units long. Since the description says that all sides are equal and there are 9 sides, the total perimeter must be 18 units.

4. No. The nonagons will leave gaps when sides are matched together. When two nonagons are placed side by side, the exterior angle formed is less than a right angle and the 140° angle of a third nonagon is too large to fit. In order not to have gaps, the nonagons must overlap and this is not reasonable when working with ceramic tiles. See below:

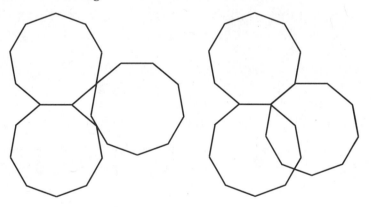

5. The angle marked in the decagon is larger than the angle marked in the nonagon. As you increase the number of sides of regular polygons, the measure of the angles increases. For example, an equilateral triangle has 60° angles, a square has 90° angles, a pentagon has 108° angles, and a hexagon has 120° angles. Also, if you cut out the nonagon and place it on top of the decagon, matching up one side, you could see that the angle of the decagon is larger.

6. The perimeter of the decagon is greater than that of the nonagon. Since the decagon has 10 equal sides that are the same length as those of the nonagon (2 units), the perimeter of the decagon is 2 units greater than the nonagon. In other words, the perimeter of the decagon is 2 × 10 = 20 units compared to the 2 × 9 = 18 units of the nonagon.

7. The area of the decagon is greater than that of the nonagon. If you put the pages together and hold them up to the light, the nonagon fits inside the decagon. Also, the decagon has 24 whole square units and 8 units that are more than one-half unit (and several units of area that are less than one-half unit). In other words, the decagon has more than 28 square units compared to the nonagon's 24 square units.

More on the Mathematics

There are two methods to geometrically determine the angles of a regular polygon.

Method 1: Draw triangles in the polygon by connecting the center of the polygon with each of its vertices. In a nonagon, nine triangles are formed (see figures below). The sum of the angles in the nine triangles of the nonagon is $9 \times 180° = 1620°$. The sum of the nine angles around the center of the nonagon is 360°. Therefore, the sum of the remaining angles (the angles of the polygon) is $1620° - 360° = 1260°$. The measure of each angle of the nonagon is $1260° \div 9 = 140°$. Similarly, for the decagon, the sum of the angles of the ten triangles is $10 \times 180° = 1800°$. The sum of the 10 angles around the center of the decagon is 360°. Therefore, the sum of the angles of the decagon is $1800° - 360° = 1440°$ and the measure of each angle of the regular decagon is $1440° \div 10 = 144°$. In general, the measure of an angle of a regular n-gon is $[n(180°) - 360°] \div n$.

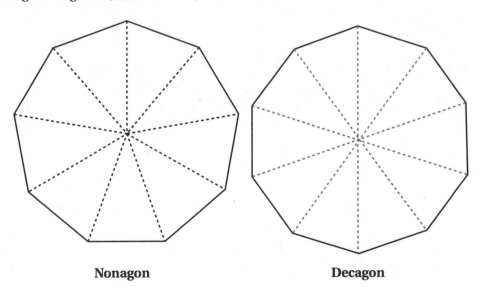

Nonagon   **Decagon**

Task

Method 2: Draw lines from one vertex of the regular n-gons to the other vertices (see figures below). There will be $n - 2$ triangles formed (7 triangles for the nonagon and 8 triangles for the decagon). Multiplying by 180° will give the total angle measurement of the triangles inside the n-gon:

$7(180°) = 1260°$ = total angle measurement of triangles inside the nonagon;

$8(180°) = 1440°$ = total angle measurement of triangles inside the decagon.

Divide the total angle measurement by the number of sides each, 9 sides for the nonagon to get 140° and 10 sides for the decagon to get 144°. In general, $\frac{[(n-2)(180°)]}{n}$ = measure of an angle in a regular n-gon.

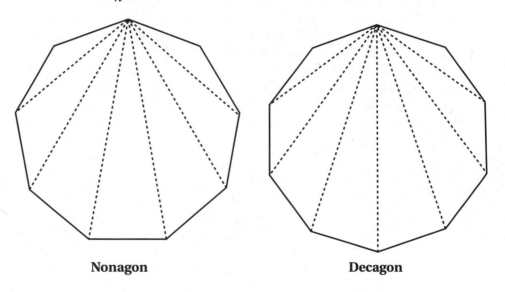

Nonagon   **Decagon**

Characterizing Performance

This section offers a characterization of student responses and provides indications of the ways in which the students were successful or unsuccessful in engaging with and completing the task. The descriptions are keyed to the *Core Elements of Performance*. Our global descriptions of student work range from "The student needs significant instruction" to "The student's work meets the essential demands of the task." Samples of student work that exemplify these descriptions of performance are included below, accompanied by commentary on central aspects of each student's response. These sample responses are representative; they may not mirror the global description of performance in all respects, being weaker in some and stronger in others.

The characterization of student responses for this task is based on these *Core Elements of Performance*:
1. Find angle measures, perimeters, and areas.
2. Reason and compare visually and geometrically about measures of two regular polygons.

Descriptions of Student Work

The student needs significant instruction.

Student engages in the task and may have some correct answers but gives nonsensical explanations.

Student A

Student A does not respond to questions 1, 2, and 5. He correctly states the perimeter of the nonagon. He does not actually state whether the nonagons will leave gaps when tiling. Student A correctly determines that the perimeter of the decagon is greater than the perimeter of the nonagon and he implies that the area of the decagon is greater than the area of the nonagon but his estimation of 64 square units for the area of the decagon is not reasonable.

The student needs some instruction.

Student demonstrates some knowledge of area, perimeter, and angle measure by correctly measuring and estimating many of the values requested for the nonagon. Student exhibits weak reasoning when comparing measures of the decagon to the nonagon and/or when determining whether the nonagon will tile without gaps or overlaps.

Student B

This student correctly measures the angle marked and estimates the area and perimeter of the nonagon. Moreover, she states that the nonagons will not make good floor tiles because "they wouldn't fit together." She correctly states that the angle of the decagon is larger than the angle of the nonagon and gives a weak explanation by saying, "Its bigger it speread out wider." She states that the perimeter of the decagon looks greater than the perimeter of the nonagon but then contradicts herself stating that she measured and got the same perimeter. Student B claims that the area of the nonagon is "probably the same" as the area of the decagon.

The student's work needs to be revised.

Student demonstrates knowledge of and ability to reason about the properties of polygons by answering most questions correctly although responses to one or two questions about reasoning may be weak or incomplete.

Student C

Student C correctly measures the angle marked and estimates the area and perimeter of the nonagon. Also, she describes how she got her answers to questions 2 and 3. Student C correctly determines that the perimeter and area of the decagon are greater than the perimeter and area of the nonagon and explains her reasoning. However, she erroneously claims that the nonagon will make good tiles and that the angle of the decagon is smaller than the angle of the nonagon.

The student's work meets the essential demands of the task.

Student demonstrates knowledge of and ability to reason about the properties of polygons by answering most questions correctly. The student's reasoning is complete and clearly explained.

Student D

Student D correctly measures the angle marked and estimates the area and perimeter of the nonagon (although he does not label his answers). He also clearly describes how he got his answers to questions 2 and 3. He determines that nonagons will not make good tiles, using a visual justification. A stronger response would have included an explanation based on the geometric properties of the shape. Student D also correctly determines that the perimeter and area of the decagon are greater than that of the nonagon and he gives a strong argument to prove it.

Polygon Measures

This problem gives you the chance to

- *find angle measurements*
- *find perimeter and area of figures*
- *compare regular polygons*

Designers are experimenting with new tile shapes for walls and floors.

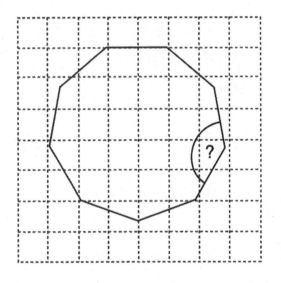

- The tile here is in the shape of a regular *nonagon*.
- The regular *nonagon* has nine equal sides and angles.

1. What is the measure of the angle marked in the figure? _____ (Use any measuring tool that will help you.)

2. Estimate the area of the nonagon. _____ Explain how you got this answer.

3. Estimate the perimeter of the nonagon. __18__ Explain how you got this answer. I estimated by considring each side as two.

4. Will nonagons make good ceramic tiles for floors and walls? Use the geometric properties of the nonagon to explain or illustrate why or why not. It depends IF you CAN cutthru them because you will have a rectangle shape room.

Designers have developed another tile shape.

■ The tile here is in the shape of a regular *decagon*.

■ A regular decagon has ten equal sides and angles.

■ The sides of this decagon are the same length as those of the nonagon.

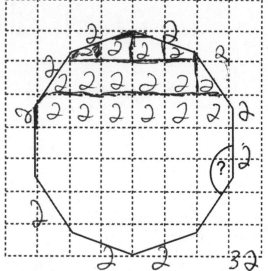

5. Without using any measuring tools, decide whether the angle marked in this decagon is larger or smaller than the angle marked in the nonagon. Explain why this is so.

6. Is the perimeter of the decagon greater, smaller, or the same as the nonagon? Explain how you know.

The perimeter of the decagon is 20
It is greater than the NONAGON
Perimeter = 2 units

7. Is the area of the decagon greater, smaller, or the same as the nonagon on the previous page? Explain your reasoning.

I estamted by counting half witch is 32
and x by 2 = 6
32 × 2 = 64   area 64 sq. units

Polygon Measures

This problem gives you the chance to
- *find angle measurements*
- *find perimeter and area of figures*
- *compare regular polygons*

Designers are experimenting with new tile shapes for walls and floors.

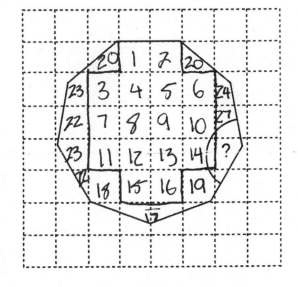

- The tile here is in the shape of a regular *nonagon*.
- The regular *nonagon* has nine equal sides and angles.

1. What is the measure of the angle marked in the figure? __140°__ (Use any measuring tool that will help you.)

2. Estimate the area of the nonagon. __24 ½__ Explain how you got this answer. I counted and matched up the squares

3. Estimate the perimeter of the nonagon. __18cm__ Explain how you got this answer. mesured with an angle ruler

4. Will nonagons make good ceramic tiles for floors and walls? Use the geometric properties of the nonagon to explain or illustrate why or why not. No they wouldn't fit together

Designers have developed another tile shape.

- The tile here is in the shape of a regular *decagon*.

- A regular decagon has ten equal sides and angles.

- The sides of this decagon are the same length as those of the nonagon.

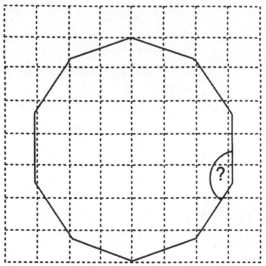

5. Without using any measuring tools, decide whether the angle marked in this decagon is larger or smaller than the angle marked in the nonagon. Explain why this is so.

Its bigger it speread out wider

6. Is the perimeter of the decagon greater, smaller, or the same as the nonagon? Explain how you know. greater because it loooks bigger but I mesured and its the same

7. Is the area of the decagon greater, smaller, or the same as the nonagon on the previous page? Explain your reasoning.

Its probably the same

Student C

Polygon Measures

This problem gives you the chance to

■ *find angle measurements*

■ *find perimeter and area of figures*

■ *compare regular polygons*

Designers are experimenting with new tile shapes for walls and floors.

■ The tile here is in the shape of a regular *nonagon*.

■ The regular *nonagon* has nine equal sides and angles.

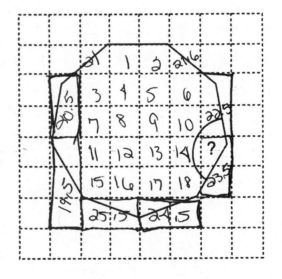

1. What is the measure of the angle marked in the figure? _____140°_____ (Use any measuring tool that will help you.)

2. Estimate the area of the nonagon. ___25.5___ Explain how you got this answer. I used a rectangle. I drew a rectangle w/ triangle taking up approx. 1/2 of the area. I figured the area of the rectangle or square and divided it in half. That was one area of that section of the nonagon. I repeated this for most of the edges for the rest I just cont

3. Estimate the perimeter of the nonagon. ___18 cm___ Explain how you got this answer. I measured each side since the square there were each 2cm in length and there are nine sides then 9 sides x 2cm each = 18 cm perimeter

4. Will nonagons make good ceramic tiles for floors and walls? Use the geometric properties of the nonagon to explain or illustrate why or why not. Yes if someone wants to take time to figure out how they fit together. It could get confusing w/ so many sides.

Designers have developed another tile shape.

■ The tile here is in the shape of a regular *decagon*.

■ A regular decagon has ten equal sides and angles.

■ The sides of this decagon are the same length as those of the nonagon.

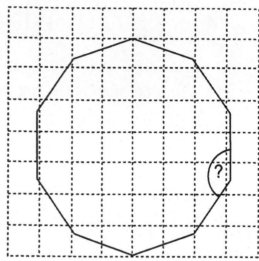

5. Without using any measuring tools, decide whether the angle marked in this decagon is larger or smaller than the angle marked in the nonagon. Explain why this is so.

    Smaller. Because the more sides a figure has, the smaller the angles have to be in order for the sides to fit together.

6. Is the perimeter of the decagon greater, smaller, or the same as the nonagon? Explain how you know.

    Greater. Because each side is 2 cm an both shapes and the dexagon has one more side so that means 2 more cm in the perimeter.

7. Is the area of the decagon greater, smaller, or the same as the nonagon on the previous page? Explain your reasoning.

    Greater. There is one more side in the dexagon. All sides are 2 cm on both figures. the figure must expand to make room for the extra side (2 cm in length)

Designers are experimenting with new tile shapes for walls and floors.

■ The tile here is in the shape of a regular *nonagon*.

■ The regular *nonagon* has nine equal sides and angles.

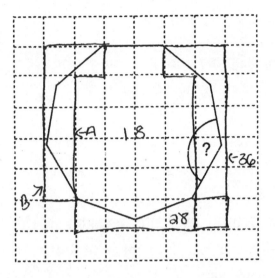

1. What is the measure of the angle marked in the figure? __140°__ (Use any measuring tool that will help you.)

2. Estimate the area of the nonagon. __24__ Explain how you got this answer. I guess that it is 24 because it must be greater than 18 (polygon A), but less than 28 (polygon B). I figure that there was much more "full" space than "empty" space, so I choose 24.

3. Estimate the perimeter of the nonagon. __18__ Explain how you got this answer. I got this because all sides are of equal length and then straight side is 2 units, so the perimeter is the length of one side (2) times the number of sides.

4. Will nonagons make good ceramic tiles for floors and walls? Use the geometric properties of the nonagon to explain or illustrate why or why not. No, since a nonagon has nine sides, and a strange shape, there will be small spaces between the tiles and where the tiles come up against the wall (or floor).

Like this:

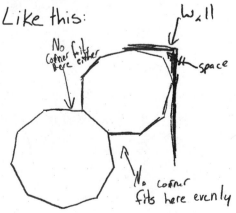

Designers have developed another tile shape.

- The tile here is in the shape of a regular *decagon*.

- A regular decagon has ten equal sides and angles.

- The sides of this decagon are the same length as those of the nonagon.

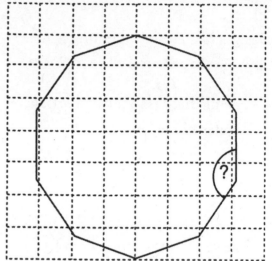

5. Without using any measuring tools, decide whether the angle marked in this decagon is larger or smaller than the angle marked in the nonagon. Explain why this is so.

The angle is larger than in the nonagon because the decagon's is closer to a straight line (180°), while the nonagon's angle is more obviously kinked.

6. Is the perimeter of the decagon greater, smaller, or the same as the nonagon? Explain how you know. It is greater because it has more sides that are, about the same length of the nonagons sides.

7. Is the area of the decagon greater, smaller, or the same as the nonagon on the previous page? Explain your reasoning.

It is going to be greater because it doesn't fit in a 30 unit² box, while the nonagon does.

Library Books

Short Task

Task Description

Students are given a bar graph depicting the number of books students have checked out from the library. They are to use the graph to answer questions. They are also asked to reason about measures of center.

Assumed Mathematical Background

It is assumed that students have had experience with interpreting graphs and using and reasoning about statistical measures.

Core Elements of Performance

- interpret a bar graph
- explain differing values for mean and median
- reason about measures of center

Circumstances

Grouping:	Students complete an individual written response.
Materials:	No special materials are needed for this task.
Estimated time:	15 minutes

Library Books

This problem gives you the chance to

- *use knowledge of statistics to analyze and interpret data in a graph*
- *justify choice of measure of center*

Nigel made a graph showing how many books were taken from the library by students in his class in the last week.

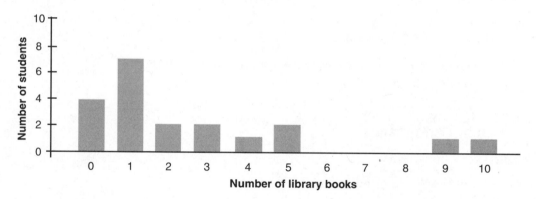

1. How many books have been taken out of the library by Nigel's class? Explain how you got your answer.

2. Mika and Jose are the only students in the class who have started working on a big report. How many books do you think that Mika and Jose have each checked out?

Mika: _____   Jose: _____

Explain your reasoning.

© *The Regents of the University of California*

3. Nigel said, "The mean number of library books that students have is 2.5." Jose said, "The median number of library books that students have is 1!"

Ms. Estaphan said, "You are both correct!"
Why are these two averages different?

4. Which average would you choose to tell what is the typical number of books checked out by the students? Explain why.

© The Regents of the University of California

Task **A Sample Solution**

11

1. Fifty books have been taken out of the library by Nigel's class.
   (0 books per student) × (4 students) = 0 books
   (1 book per student) × (7 students) = 7 books
   (2 books per student) × (2 students) = 4 books
   (3 books per student) × (2 students) = 6 books
   (4 books per student) × (1 student) = 4 books
   (5 books per student) × (2 students) = 10 books
   (6 books per student) × (0 students) = 0 books
   (7 books per student) × (0 students) = 0 books
   (8 books per student) × (0 students) = 0 books
   (9 books per student) × (1 student) = 9 books
   (10 books per student) × (1 student) = 10 books
   Total = 50 books

2. Mika may have checked out 9 books and Jose 10 books or vice versa. It is reasonable to assume this since they are the only ones working on reports.

3. The mean and median are different because they are two different measures of center, two different types of average. The mean is the number of books each student would have if books were distributed and each student had the same number of books. To find the mean number of books you could divide the total number of books by the number of students: 50 books ÷ 20 students = 2.5 books per student.

   The median is the number of books that half the class has more than (or equal to) and half the class has less than (or equal to). To find the median, one could list in order the number of books checked out by the students. Since there are an even number of students in this class, 20, halfway between the 10th and 11th entry is the median. Since both the 10th and 11th entries are 1 book, 1 is the median. (If the middle two entries were different amounts, then the median would be halfway between them.)

4. Response A: I would choose 2.5 books as the typical number of books checked out because the mean spreads everything out evenly. Thus, 2.5 represents the number of books each student would have if the books were equally distributed.

   Response B: I would choose 1 book as the typical number of books checked out because 1 book represents the middle of the data set. Half the students have 1 or fewer books checked out and half the students have 1 or more books checked out. Also, the two students who checked out 9 and 10 books skewed the mean upward. In this class they are like outliers.

Characterizing Performance

This section offers a characterization of student responses and provides indications of the ways in which the students were successful or unsuccessful in engaging with and completing the task. The descriptions are keyed to the *Core Elements of Performance.* Our global descriptions of student work range from "The student needs significant instruction" to "The student's work meets the essential demands of the task." Samples of student work that exemplify these descriptions of performance are included below, accompanied by commentary on central aspects of each student's response. These sample responses are *representative;* they may not mirror the global description of performance in all respects, being weaker in some and stronger in others.

The characterization of student responses for this task is based on these *Core Elements of Performance:*

1. Interpret a bar graph.
2. Explain differing values for mean and median.
3. Reason about measures of center.

Descriptions of Student Work

The student needs significant instruction.

Student engages in the task, but does not correctly explain how the total number of books was determined and shows no reasoning about statistical measures.

Student A

Student A's responses are incorrect. The student shows no understanding of how to interpret a bar graph, nor how to analyze statistical measures.

The student needs some instruction.

Student adequately explains how he/she determined the total number of books, but does not adequately define mean and median or the choice of which average better represents the typical number of books borrowed.

Task

11

Student B

Student B sufficiently explains how he arrived at 50 total books checked out of the library. Student B, however, does not define mean and median in question 3, nor does he select and justify why mean or median is a better choice for describing the typical number of books checked out.

The student's work needs to be revised.

Student adequately explains how he/she determined the total number of books. Student also shows some understanding of measures of center by either adequately defining median and mean *OR* by providing adequate justification for choosing which average represents the typical number of books.

Student C

Student C shows how she determined the total number of books. Student C also adequately defines both mean and median. However, she does not provide any justification for her choice of mean as the better measure except for stating "it is more accurate."

The student's work meets the essential demands of the task.

Student shows how he/she determined total number of books. Student shows understanding of measures of center by adequately defining median and mean *AND* student provides adequate justification for choosing which average best represents the typical number of books.

Student D

Student D shows how the correct total number of books was determined. Student D adequately defines median and mode and sufficiently justifies the choice of mean to represent the typical number of books. In general conversation "average" is often used to signify "mean." Therefore, Student D does not commit a serious error when implying that the median is not an average.

Student A

Library Books

This problem gives you the chance to
- *use knowledge of statistics to analyze and interpret data in a graph*
- *justify choice of measure of center*

Nigel made a graph showing how many books were taken from the library by students in his class in the last week.

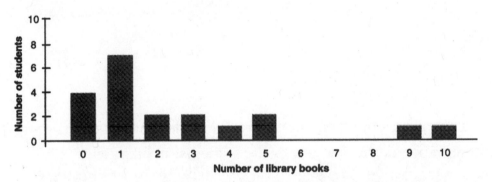

1. How many books have been taken out of the library by Nigel's class? Explain how you got your answer. 24 students
   I got that by Adding the books to the students.

2. Mika and Jose are the only students in the class who have started working on a big report. How many books do you think that Mika and Jose have each checked out?

   Mika: 3 books   Jose: 4 books
   Explain your reasoning.
   I took 1/3 Away and got 3 books For Mika and
   4 books For Jose.

3. Nigel said, "The mean number of library books that students have is 2.5." Jose said, "The median number of library books that students have is 1!"

Ms. Estaphan said, "You are both correct!"
Why are these two averages different?

Because the lowest Number is 1 and the Adverge is 2.5 which is the Same on scale of 1–10.

4. Which average would you choose to tell what is the typical number of books checked out by the students? Explain why.

The meAN, it is easier to Find because it is Finding the averge of your amont.

Student B

Library Books

This problem gives you the chance to

■ *use knowledge of statistics to analyze and interpret data in a graph*

■ *justify choice of measure of center*

Nigel made a graph showing how many books were taken from the library by students in his class in the last week.

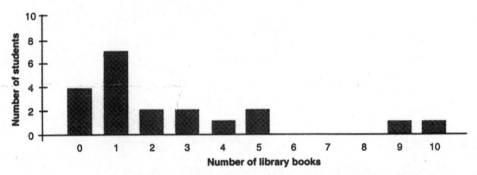

1. How many books have been taken out of the library by Nigel's class? Explain how you got your answer. 50 Books, I counted each of the squares but if there was 7 people that took out 1 Book that's 7 books and that's what I did for all of them.

2. Mika and Jose are the only students in the class who have started working on a big report. How many books do you think that Mika and Jose have each checked out?

Mika: _____10_____   Jose: _____9_____

Explain your reasoning. Because They're doing a big report so I thought they were the ones that checked out the most books.

3. Nigel said, "The mean number of library books that students have is 2.5." Jose said, "The median number of library books that students have is 1!"

Ms. Estaphan said, "You are both correct!"
Why are these two averages different?

They're both correct because if you count the zeros you would get 1 but if you don't count the zeroes you get 2.5

4. Which average would you choose to tell what is the typical number of books checked out by the students? Explain why.

2.5 Because I don't think you would count zero because those aren't any books but if you want the whole class, I would pick 1 because your telling how many books the whole class took out.

Library Books

This problem gives you the chance to

■ *use knowledge of statistics to analyze and interpret data in a graph*

■ *justify choice of measure of center*

Nigel made a graph showing how many books were taken from the library by students in his class in the last week.

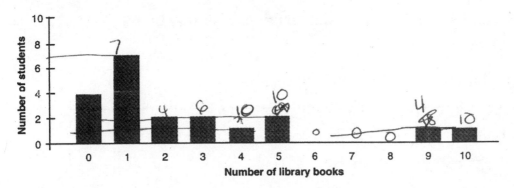

1. How many books have been taken out of the library by Nigel's class? Explain how you got your answer.

30
7
4
6
4
10
0
9
+10

50

(50)

4 people took out o books = 0
7 people took out 1 book = 7 books
2 people took out 2 books = 4
2 people took out 3 books = 6
1 person took out 4 books = 4
2 people took out 5 books = 10
No one took out 6,7, or 8 books = 0
1 person took out 9 books ——— 9
1 person took out 10 books ——— 10

2. Mika and Jose are the only students in the class who have started working on a big report. How many books do you think that Mika and Jose have each checked out?

Mika: ~~3~~ 9 books   Jose: ~~8~~ 10 books

Explain your reasoning. Because The Probly need a lot of Books for there report.

3. Nigel said, "The mean number of library books that students have is 2.5." Jose said, "The median number of library books that students have is 1!"

Ms. Estaphan said, "You are both correct!"

Why are these two averages different? Because in the mean you divide The Total number of books by The Total number of Kids And the ~~mean~~ median isThe middle of all of The info

4. Which average would you choose to tell what is the typical number of books checked out by the students? Explain why.

The mean Because it is more accurate

Library Books

This problem gives you the chance to

- *use knowledge of statistics to analyze and interpret data in a graph*
- *justify choice of measure of center*

Nigel made a graph showing how many books were taken from the library by students in his class in the last week.

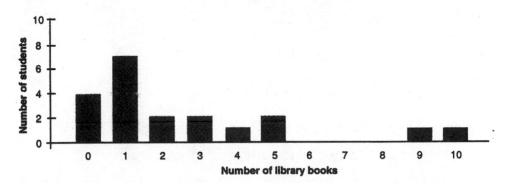

1. How many books have been taken out of the library by Nigel's class? Explain how you got your answer. 50 books total

number of books → x1 x2 x3 x4 x5 x6 x7 x8 x9 x10

number of students → x7 x2 x2 x1 x2 x0 x0 x0 x1 x1

0 +7 +4 +6 +4 +10 +0 +0 +0 +9 +10

1 2 3 4 5 6 7 8 9 10

2. Mika and José are the only students in the class who have started working on a big report. How many books do you think that Mika and Jose have each checked out?

Mika: _____9_____   Jose: _____10_____

Explain your reasoning. Because only one person checked out 9 or 10 books and usually people do not check out that many books. They were out liers because they checked out more books than any one else so they must be doing the reports

3. Nigel said, "The mean number of library books that students have is 2.5." Jose said, "The median number of library books that students have is 1!"

Ms. Estaphan said, "You are both correct!"
Why are these two averages different?

Because the mean is the over all amount. So if you give the same amount of books to everyone they would have 2.5 ~~a~~ books and the median is the middle of the data.

4. Which average would you choose to tell what is the typical number of books checked out by the students? Explain why.

The mean because it shows an average and the median only tells the middle. The mean would tell me what is typical because it would even everything out and tell me what is typical.

Continue a pattern.
Describe a pattern.
Generalize a rule.

Pat's Pattern

Short Task

Task Description

Students are given a sequence of figures. They draw the next figure, describe the pattern of figures in words, and generalize the pattern symbolically.

Assumed Mathematical Background

It is assumed that students have had experience working with and generalizing patterns.

Core Elements of Performance

- continue a geometric and numeric pattern
- generalize the pattern in words and symbols

Circumstances

Grouping:	Students complete an individual written response.
Materials:	No special materials are needed for this task.
Estimated time:	15 minutes

Acknowledgment

We thank Quasar for their work on this task.

Pat's Pattern

This problem gives you the chance to

■ *analyze, continue, describe, and generalize a pattern*

Pat's teacher asked him to look at the pattern below and draw the figure that would come next.

Figure 1   **Figure 2**   **Figure 3**   **Figure 4**

Pat does not know how to find the next figure.

1. Draw the next figure for Pat.

© The Regents of the University of California

2. Write a description for Pat telling him how you knew which figure comes next. Make sure that Pat can understand how to continue the pattern himself.

3. Write a rule that describes how to draw any Figure *n*.

© The Regents of the University of California

A Sample Solution

1.

   Figure 5

2. Each figure has 3 rows of dots. As the pattern continues, one dot is added to each row from the previous figure. Each row of dots must be centered, forming a symmetrical shape.

3. Figure 1 has one dot in the top row, Figure 2 has 2 dots in the top row, Figure 3 has 3 dots in the top row, and so on. Therefore, Figure n will have n dots in the top row. In each figure, the middle row has one dot more than the top row and the bottom row has one dot more than the middle row. Therefore, Figure n will look like this:

   • • • • • • • … • • • • n dots
   • • • • • • • … • • • • • $n + 1$ dots
   • • • • • • … • • • • • • $n + 2$ dots

Characterizing Performance

This section offers a characterization of student responses and provides indications of the ways in which the students were successful or unsuccessful in engaging with and completing the task. The descriptions are keyed to the *Core Elements of Performance*. Our global descriptions of student work range from "The student needs significant instruction" to "The student's work meets the essential demands of the task." Samples of student work that exemplify these descriptions of performance are included below, accompanied by commentary on central aspects of each student's response. These sample responses are *representative;* they may not mirror the global description of performance in all respects, being weaker in some and stronger in others.

The characterization of student responses for this task is based on these *Core Elements of Performance:*

1. Continue a geometric and numeric pattern.
2. Generalize the pattern in words and symbols.

Descriptions of Student Work

The student needs significant instruction.

Student draws a correct figure in question 1, but description in question 2 is insufficient (for Pat to know how to draw the next figure) *AND* the rule in question 3 is incorrect, nonsensical, or is not expressed in general terms.

Student A

Student A draws Figure 5 correctly. Her description in question 2 mentions adding a dot only to the bottom row and her statement "and only went up three rows" is not enough to imply that one dot was added to each of the three rows in the figure. Student A's description of how to draw any Figure *n* is incorrect.

The student needs some instruction.

Student draws a correct figure in question 1 and gives a sufficient description in question 2, but the rule in question 3 is incorrect, nonsensical, or is not expressed in general terms.

Task

12

Student B

Student B draws Figure 5 correctly. His description "extend each line out one more dot" is sufficient. Student B's rule in question 3 is incorrect.

The student's work needs to be revised.

Student draws a correct figure in question 1 and gives a sufficient description in question 2 *AND* offers a general rule in question 3, but the rule either depends on knowledge of the previous figure or there are some minor errors.

Student C

Student C draws Figure 5 correctly. Her description in question 2 is sufficient to draw the next figure. The student's rule for question 3 is based on the previous figure. The student is not explicitly clear what she means by "1st row + 1," but given her description in question 2, it is reasonable to infer that she is generalizing with a recursive rule, referring to previous figures.

The student's work meets the essential demands of the task.

Student draws a correct figure in question 1, gives a good description in question 2, and gives a correct, general, and symbolic rule in question 3 in terms of n.

Student D

Student D draws Figure 5 correctly. Student D's description in question 2 is correct. The student gives a rule in question 3 that is symbolic, correct, and in terms of n.

Pat's Pattern

This problem gives you the chance to

■ *analyze, continue, describe, and generalize a pattern*

Pat's teacher asked him to look at the pattern below and draw the figure that would come next.

Figure 1   **Figure 2**   **Figure 3**   **Figure 4**

Pat does not know how to find the next figure.

1. Draw the next figure for Pat.

Student A

2. Write a description for Pat telling him how you knew which figure comes next. Make sure that Pat can understand how to continue the pattern himself.

Well, they just added an extra dot on the bottom row, and only went up three rows.

3. Write a rule that describes how to draw any Figure n.

Start from three dots and just keep adding an extra dot. to the bottom row and the figure should stay similar to the rest of the figures.

Pat's Pattern

This problem gives you the chance to

■ *analyze, continue, describe, and generalize a pattern*

Pat's teacher asked him to look at the pattern below and draw the figure that would come next.

Figure 1   **Figure 2**   **Figure 3**   **Figure 4**

Pat does not know how to find the next figure.

1. Draw the next figure for Pat.

2. Write a description for Pat telling him how you knew which figure comes next. Make sure that Pat can understand how to continue the pattern himself.

extend each line out one more dot. So that there is one more dot in each row then there was before.

3. Write a rule that describes how to draw any Figure *n*.

F=N+1

Pat's Pattern

This problem gives you the chance to

■ *analyze, continue, describe, and generalize a pattern*

Pat's teacher asked him to look at the pattern below and draw the figure that would come next.

Figure 1   **Figure 2**   **Figure 3**   **Figure 4**

Pat does not know how to find the next figure.

1. Draw the next figure for Pat.

2. Write a description for Pat telling him how you knew which figure comes next. Make sure that Pat can understand how to continue the pattern himself.

On each horizontal line of dots, the next pattern has added one more dot. There are always three rows of dots,

3. Write a rule that describes how to draw any Figure *n*.

n - 1st row + 1
n - 2nd row + 1
n - 3rd row + 1

Pat's Pattern

This problem gives you the chance to

■ *analyze, continue, describe, and generalize a pattern*

Pat's teacher asked him to look at the pattern below and draw the figure that would come next.

Figure 1　　**Figure 2**　　**Figure 3**　　**Figure 4**

Pat does not know how to find the next figure.

1. Draw the next figure for Pat.

5 = • • ● • •
6 = • • • ● • •
7 = • • • ○ • • •

2. Write a description for Pat telling him how you knew which figure comes next. Make sure that Pat can understand how to continue the pattern himself.

Add one (1) dot to each line

3. Write a rule that describes how to draw any Figure *n*.

First line | second line | third line

$$N = N \mid N+1 \mid N+2$$

Reason about factors and multiples.
Communicate reasoning.

Secret Number

Short Task

Task Description

Students are given clues about Juanita's "secret number." They judge whether each successive clue provides enough information to find the number and explain why or why not. They also write clues for finding a different secret number.

Assumed Mathematical Background

It is assumed that students have had experience with factors, multiples, and prime numbers.

Core Elements of Performance

- reason about factors and multiples
- communicate mathematical reasoning

Circumstances

Grouping:	Students complete an individual written response.
Materials:	No special materials are needed for this task.
Estimated time:	15 minutes

Secret Number

> ## This problem gives you the chance to
> - *reason about factors, multiples, and other number properties*
> - *communicate mathematical reasoning*

Juanita has a secret number. Read her clues and then answer the questions that follow.

Juanita says, "Clue 1: My secret number is a factor of 60."

1. Can you tell what Juanita's secret number is? Explain your reasoning.

2. Daren said that Juanita's number must also be a factor of 120. Do you agree or disagree with Daren? Explain your reasoning.

3. Malcolm says that Juanita's number must also be a factor of 15. Do you agree or disagree with Malcolm? Explain your reasoning.

4. What is the smallest Juanita's number could be? Explain.

© The Regents of the University of California

5. What is the largest Juanita's number could be? Explain.

Suppose for Juanita's second clue she says, "Clue 2: My number is prime."

6. Can the class guess her number and be certain? Explain your reasoning.

Suppose for Juanita's third clue she says, "Clue 3: 15 is a multiple of my secret number."

7. Now can you tell what her number is? Explain your reasoning.

8. Your secret number is 36. Write a series of *interesting clues* using factors, multiples, and other number properties needed for somebody else to identify your number.

© The Regents of the University of California

Task 13 **A Sample Solution**

1. No. Students cannot be certain of Juanita's secret number. It could be any of the factors of 60: 1, 2, 3, 4, 5, 6, 10, 12, 15, 20, 30, 60.

2. Students should agree with Daren. Since 60 is a factor of 120 (60 × 2 = 120), and Juanita's secret number is a factor of 60, then her number must also be a factor of 120.

3. Students should disagree with Malcolm. Juanita's number is not necessarily a factor of 15 since 20, 30, and 60 are all factors of 60 and yet they are not factors of 15.

4. The smallest number that Juanita's secret number could be is 1, because 1 is the smallest factor of any number.

5. The largest number that Juanita's secret number could be is 60. A number's largest possible factor is always itself.

6. No, the class still cannot be certain of Juanita's number because 2, 3, and 5 are all prime factors of 60.

7. No, the class still cannot tell because 15 is a multiple of 3 and 5, both of which are prime factors of 60.

8. One possible solution: My secret number is a factor of 72. My secret number is also a perfect square with more than one digit.

   Another possible solution: My secret number is a multiple of 2 and 3. It is greater than 30 and less than 40.

   Another possible solution: My secret number is a multiple of 12 greater than 12. It is a factor of 72. It is not a multiple of 24.

Characterizing Performance

This section offers a characterization of student responses and provides indications of the ways in which the students were successful or unsuccessful in engaging with and completing the task. The descriptions are keyed to the *Core Elements of Performance*. Our global descriptions of student work range from "The student needs significant instruction" to "The student's work meets the essential demands of the task." Samples of student work that exemplify these descriptions of performance are included below, accompanied by commentary on central aspects of each student's response. These sample responses are *representative;* they may not mirror the global description of performance in all respects, being weaker in some and stronger in others.

The characterization of student responses for this task is based on these *Core Elements of Performance:*
1. Reason about factors and multiples.
2. Communicate mathematical reasoning.

Descriptions of Student Work

The student needs significant instruction.

Student engages in the task, but demonstrates little understanding of factors and multiples.

No student examples at this level.

The student needs some instruction.

Student demonstrates some understanding of factors and multiples by answering some of the questions correctly, but others are answered incorrectly and explanations are weak or inadequate. In question 8, student does not give sufficient clues or one clue "gives away" the number.

Task

Student A

Student A correctly answers questions 1, 2, and 4, but his reasoning is weak. For question 6 he is correct when he says "no," but his explanation is inadequate. He says there are "a lot of numbers with a prime factor of 60" without stating which numbers he is referring to. In question 8, Student A "gives away" his secret number with his third clue, "it is twice the size of 18." Unlike the clues given for Juanita's secret number, his clues tell the secret number.

The student's work needs to be revised.

Student demonstrates understanding of factors and multiples by answering most questions correctly and by providing some clear and complete explanations. In question 8 student does not give sufficient clues or one clue "gives away" the number.

Student B

Student B answers questions 1–5 correctly. His responses to questions 6 and 7 are correct. Yet, in both, he has left out one of the prime factors of 60. Student B's explanations are mostly clear and precise. In question 8, he gives a number of clues. However, they are insufficient to identify the secret number 36 absolutely; 12 also fits his clues.

The student's work meets the essential demands of the task.

Student answers all questions correctly, provides clear and complete explanations, and gives sufficient clues to identify 36 in question 8 without "giving it away" (minor mistakes are okay).

Student C

Student C answers almost all questions correctly and provides good explanations. For example, she lists all the factors of 60 and offers a counterexample when disagreeing with Malcolm. She makes an error in question 6, forgetting 2 as a prime factor of 60. In response to question 8, Student C gives clues that enable the reader to guess her secret number precisely and all her clues are needed.

Secret Number

This problem gives you the chance to

- *reason about factors, multiples, and other number properties*
- *communicate mathematical reasoning*

Juanita has a secret number. Read her clues and then answer the questions that follow.

Juanita says, "Clue 1: My secret number is a factor of 60."

1. Can you tell what Juanita's secret number is? Explain your reasoning. No
   Because theresalot of factors to 60

2. Daren said that Juanita's number must also be a factor of 120.
   Do you agree or disagree with Daren? Explain your reasoning. yes
   Because 120 is twice 60.

   60
   150

3. Malcolm says that Juanita's number must also be a factor of 15. Do you agree or disagree with Malcolm? Explain your reasoning. yes
   Becaus 15 x 4 is 60.

4. What is the smallest Juanita's number could be? Explain. it could
   Be 1 Because its a factor to 60, 120, and 15, and 4.

5. What is the largest Juanita's number could be? Explain. iS 240
Because its twice $20 and a numbers
factor onlygoes to half itself.

Suppose for Juanita's second clue she says, "Clue 2:   My
number is prime."

6. Can the class guess her number and be certain? Explain your
reasoning. NO Because a lot of numbers
with a ~~factor of~~
Prime factor of 60.

Suppose for Juanita's third clue she says, "Clue 3:   15 is a
multiple of my secret number."

7. Now can you tell what her number is? Explain your
reasoning. Yes it is 2 Because its the
only number how is a factor to 60
Mutiplied By 15.

8. Your secret number is 36. Write a series of *interesting clues*
using factors, multiples, and other number properties
needed for somebody else to identify your number.

36 ① my number is a
multiple of 6.
② It is a factor of of 72
③ it is twice the size of ⒅

Secret Number

This problem gives you the chance to

▪ *reason about factors, multiples, and other number properties*

▪ *communicate mathematical reasoning*

Juanita has a secret number. Read her clues and then answer the questions that follow.

Juanita says, "Clue 1:   My secret number is a factor of 60."

1. **Can you tell what Juanita's secret number is? Explain your reasoning.** No because it doesn't give enough information because it could be any of 60's factors, and there are a lot of factors of 60.

2. **Daren said that Juanita's number must also be a factor of 120.**

   Do you agree or disagree with Daren? Explain your reasoning. Yes because 60 is a factor of 120 and is half So it would have the same factors.

3. **Malcolm says that Juanita's number must also be a factor of 15. Do you agree or disagree with Malcolm? Explain your reasoning.** No because 4 is a factor of 60 and it isn't a factor of 15 neither is 2 or 6.

4. **What is the smallest Juanita's number could be? Explain.** 1 because it is the smallest factor that is of 60.

5. **What is the largest Juanita's number could be? Explain.**

60 because you could multiply it by 1 and get 60.

Suppose for Juanita's second clue she says, "Clue 2: My number is prime."

6. **Can the class guess her number and be certain? Explain your reasoning.** No because there is two prime numbers that are factors of 60.

Suppose for Juanita's third clue she says, "Clue 3: 15 is a multiple of my secret number."

7. **Now can you tell what her number is? Explain your reasoning.** Yes it is 5 because 5 is a prime and it has 15 as a multiple.

8. **Your secret number is 36. Write a series of *interesting clues* using factors, multiples, and other number properties needed for somebody else to identify your number.**

My number is a factor of 72. My number is composite. One of its multiples is 108. Some of its factors are 2, and 12.

Secret Number

This problem gives you the chance to

- *reason about factors, multiples, and other number properties*
- *communicate mathematical reasoning*

Juanita has a secret number. Read her clues and then answer the questions that follow.

Juanita says, "Clue 1:   My secret number is a factor of 60."

1. Can you tell what Juanita's secret number is? Explain your reasoning. Juanita's number could be 1,2,3,4,5,6,10,12,15,20,30,60 Because all of those numbers are factors of 60.

2. Daren said that Juanita's number must also be a factor of 120. Do you agree or disagree with Daren? Explain your reasoning. I agree because if it is a factor of 60 it must be a factor of 120 because 60 in a factor of 120.

3. Malcolm says that Juanita's number must also be a factor of 15. Do you agree or disagree with Malcolm? Explain your reasoning. I Disagree because 4 is not a factor of 15 but it is a factor of 60.

4. What is the smallest Juanita's number could be? Explain. The smallest number it could be would be 1 because all the other factors are higher than 1

5. What is the largest Juanita's number could be? Explain.

60 because it is bigger than all the other factors.

Suppose for Juanita's second clue she says, "Clue 2: My number is prime."

6. Can the class guess her number and be certain? Explain your reasoning.

The class can either guess 5 or 3 because those are the only numbers that have 1 and itself as factors.

Suppose for Juanita's third clue she says, "Clue 3: 15 is a multiple of my secret number."

7. Now can you tell what her number is? Explain your reasoning.

No because 5×3=15. They both have 15 as their multiple

8. Your secret number is 36. Write a series of *interesting clues* using factors, multiples, and other number properties needed for somebody else to identify your number.

My secret number is a factor of 72.
My secret number is a multiple of 9.
My secret number has a 4 as a factor.
My secret number is a square.

Overview

Represent data in a graph.
Select a measure of center.
Justify choice for measure of center.

Vet Club

Short Task

Task Description

Students are given a list of data showing the number of pets owned by each student in the Vet Club. Students represent the data in a graph and decide what is the typical number of pets owned by a member.

Assumed Mathematical Background

It is assumed that students have had experience making and interpreting graphs and finding and interpreting measures of center.

Core Elements of Performance

- organize and represent data in a graph
- choose a representative statistic and justify the choice

Circumstances

Grouping:	Students complete an individual written response.
Materials:	graph paper
Estimated time:	15 minutes

Vet Club

This problem gives you the chance to

- *organize and represent data*
- *choose an appropriate statistic*
- *justify reasoning*

Jenny is writing a newsletter article about the members of the Future Veterinarians Club. She asked each of the members: "What pets live in your house?" Her notes look like this:

B. J.	none	J. M.	1 dog
A. P.	1 dog and 1 cat	J. Z.	none
K. K.	2 dogs	S. F.	3 cats
R. B.	1 bird, 1 dog, and 4 goldfish	E. P.	none
G. L.	1 dog	K. B.	1 bird
W. F.	none	S. L.	2 dogs, 1 bird, and 2 fish
J. A.	1 rabbit	D. L.	6 fish

© The Regents of the University of California

1. Your job is to prepare a graph to go with Jenny's article. Organize the information from her notes into a graph that will show how many of her friends have no pets, one pet, two pets, and so on.

Jenny plans to title the article:

**Typical Future Veterinarians Club
Member Has __?__ House Pets**

2. What number should Jenny put in the blank? _____

3. Explain why the number you chose is the best number to complete the headline.

© The Regents of the University of California

Task **A Sample Solution**

14

1. The critical feature of the graph is that one variable or axis needs to be "Number of house pets" and the other variable or axis needs to be "Frequency or number of club members." Any graph that organizes the data in a clear way that is easy to analyze is acceptable. For example:

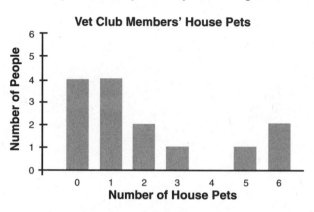

Vet Club Members' House Pets

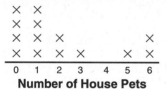

2. Jenny should fill in the blank with either number 1 or number 2.

3. **Response A:** I chose the number 1 because the median of the data is 1. Half the club members have 1 pet or less and half of them have 1 pet or more. Although there are members with up to six pets, more members have 0 or 1 pet than any other number of pets (0 and 1 are the modes). Most members have at least 1 pet, so I don't think 0 is typical. I think 1 is the best choice.

   Response B: I chose the number 2 because the mean of the data is 2. If you add up the total number of pets and you get 28, divide by the total number of members, which is 14 and you get a mean of 2. The middle of the spread of the data is 3, but the data is much more concentrated around 0, 1, and 2, than around 3, 4, 5, and 6. So, this supports a choice of 2 as well. Although half of the members have 0 or 1 pet, there are also a lot of members with more pets, so 1 can be misleading. I think 2 is the best choice.

Characterizing Performance

This section offers a characterization of student responses and provides indications of the ways in which the students were successful or unsuccessful in engaging with and completing the task. The descriptions are keyed to the *Core Elements of Performance.* Our global descriptions of student work range from "The student needs significant instruction" to "The student's work meets the essential demands of the task." Samples of student work that exemplify these descriptions of performance are included below, accompanied by commentary on central aspects of each student's response. These sample responses are *representative;* they may not mirror the global description of performance in all respects, being weaker in some and stronger in others.

The characterization of student responses for this task is based on these *Core Elements of Performance:*
1. Organize and represent data in a graph.
2. Choose a representative statistic and justify the choice.

Descriptions of Student Work

The student needs significant instruction.

Student engages in the task but neither represents the data in a graph or line plot nor makes a reasonable and/or justified choice of a typical statistic.

Student A

Student A does not organize the information into a graph. She does not summarize the data in any way and states that the total number of pets, 28, is typical.

The student needs some instruction.

Student represents the data in a line plot or graph but fails to make a reasonable and/or justified choice of a typical statistic.

Student B

Student B correctly organizes the information into a scatter plot, but does not choose a summary statistic to represent what is typical.

Task

The student's work needs to be revised.

Student represents the data in a graph or line plot, chooses a typical statistic, *AND* student's justification demonstrates some reasoning about statistical measures, but is weak (for example, student only gives a definition of the summary statistic used). The graph may be somewhat incomplete.

Student C

Student C correctly organizes the information into a scatter plot, although he does not title his graph nor label the axes. He chooses a summary statistic to represent the data and offers some explanation, but his justification is weak. His work suggests that he might be thinking about 1 as the mode and informally thinking about median, but one cannot be sure by the limited explanation given.

The student's work meets the essential demands of the task.

Student represents the data in a complete and clear graph or line plot *AND* student's justification for choosing a typical statistic is strong.

Student D

Student D represents the information in a correct and clearly labeled bar graph. The student chooses "2" as the typical statistic and provides strong justification. Student D does not simply define or explain how to find the mean, but reasons about both the mean and the spread of the data.

1. Your job is to prepare a graph to go with Jenny's article. Organize the information from her notes into a graph that will show how many of her friends have no pets, one pet, two pets, and so on.

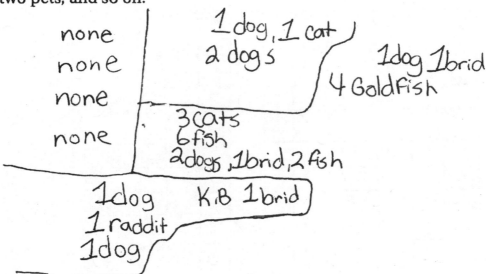

Jenny plans to title the article:

Typical Future Veterinarians Club
Member Has __?__ House Pets

2. What number should Jenny put in the blank? __28__

3. Explain why the number you chose is the best number to complete the headline. *becaus thats how many are in the club.*

1. Your job is to prepare a graph to go with Jenny's article. Organize the information from her notes into a graph that will show how many of her friends have no pets, one pet, two pets, and so on.

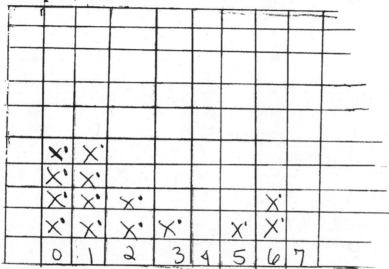

Number of Pet Each

Jenny plans to title the article:

Typical Future Veterinarians Club

Member Has __?__ House Pets

2. What number should Jenny put in the blank? _28_

3. Explain why the number you chose is the best number to complete the headline.

    Because if you add up the numbers of pets altogether there are 28 pets.

1. Your job is to prepare a graph to go with Jenny's article. Organize the information from her notes into a graph that will show how many of her friends have no pets, one pet, two pets, and so on.

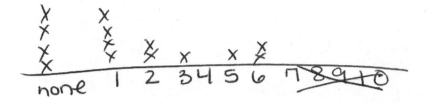

Jenny plans to title the article:

Typical Future Veterinarians Club
Member Has ＿?＿ House Pets

2. What number should Jenny put in the blank? ＿＿1＿＿

3. Explain why the number you chose is the best number to complete the headline.

I think it is the best # because there is 4 people that have 1 pet and the others either have none or 1 person either has 3,5,6, pets.

1. Your job is to prepare a graph to go with Jenny's article. Organize the information from her notes into a graph that will show how many of her friends have no pets, one pet, two pets, and so on.

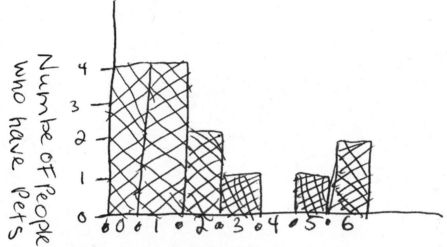

Jenny plans to title the article:

Typical Future Veterinarians Club

Member Has __?__ House Pets

2. What number should Jenny put in the blank? ____2____

3. Explain why the number you chose is the best number to complete the headline.

   Some of the people have 5 or 6 pets, but more people have 0 or 1 pets. About midway between these groups is the number 2. Also if you Average the number of pets people has you get 2. So the typical person has 2 pets

15

Reason about rectangles. Find dimensions of rectangles with a fixed perimeter.

Framing Materials

Short Task

Task Description

Students are shown a piece of framing material with fixed lengths marked on it and are asked to determine whether it can form a rectangle. Then students describe rectangular arrangements of tiles that can be framed by a fixed length of material.

Assumed Mathematical Background

It is assumed that students have had experience with rectangles and finding perimeter.

Core Elements of Performance

- apply properties of rectangles to determine if a given frame can form a rectangular shape

- explain reasoning

- find all possible whole-number dimensions for rectangles with a fixed perimeter

Circumstances

Grouping:	Students complete an individual written response.
Materials:	grid paper and rulers
Estimated time:	10 minutes

Framing Materials

This problem gives you the chance to

- *apply properties of rectangles*
- *explain your reasoning*
- *find dimensions of rectangles*

1. Suppose a 60-inch strip of framing material was bent into segments of 10 inches, 10 inches, 20 inches, and 20 inches, in that order. Can this strip of metal, bent at these marks, form a rectangular frame? Explain why or why not.

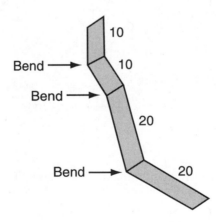

Bend → 10
10
Bend →
20
Bend → 20

2. You are given several 60-inch strips of framing material. Each strip is to be used to make a frame that encloses 1-inch square tiles. Give the dimensions of all the possible rectangular frames that can be made using the strips.

© *The Regents of the University of California*

A Sample Solution

1. The strips of metal cannot be bent at the marks to form a rectangle because opposite sides would not be the same lengths. If the material was bent at the given marks to form a closed shape, the angles would not be right angles. If you put the two ends together, a kite shape is formed.

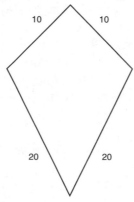

2. All rectangles with perimeters of 60 inches are possible. Since the tiles are 1 inch on each side, the dimensions must be in whole-inch units.

One can make an organized list of all possible rectangles. In a rectangle 1 tile wide, the two widths of the rectangle would use 2 inches of the 60 inches of framing material, 1 inch for each side. 58 inches is left for the lengths. $58 \div 2 = 29$, so the rectangle must be 29 inches long.

The next rectangle would have a width of two tiles (2 inches), taking up 4 inches of the framing material for the two widths. 56 inches remains, allowing for a length of 28 tiles ($56 \div 2 = 28$).

Continuing in this fashion, you can generate the following list of possibilities (the units of length and width are number of tiles as well as inches):

Width	Length	Perimeter	Width	Length	Perimeter
1	29	60	9	21	60
2	28	60	10	20	60
3	27	60	11	19	60
4	26	60	12	18	60
5	25	60	13	17	60
6	24	60	14	16	60
7	23	60	15	15	60
8	22	60			

Task **15**

Characterizing Performance

This section offers a characterization of student responses and provides indications of the ways in which the students were successful or unsuccessful in engaging with and completing the task. The descriptions are keyed to the *Core Elements of Performance.* Our global descriptions of student work range from "The student needs significant instruction" to "The student's work meets the essential demands of the task." Samples of student work that exemplify these descriptions of performance are included below, accompanied by commentary on central aspects of each student's response. These sample responses are *representative;* they may not mirror the global description of performance in all respects, being weaker in some and stronger in others.

The characterization of student responses for this task is based on these *Core Elements of Performance:*
1. Apply properties of rectangles to determine if a given frame can form a rectangular shape.
2. Explain reasoning.
3. Find all possible whole-number dimensions for rectangles with a fixed perimeter.

Descriptions of Student Work

The student's work cannot be assessed.

Student A

Student A addresses all questions as if "rectangle" read "equilateral triangle." Within this context, his responses are correct. Student A's responses provide no evidence of reasoning about rectangles and therefore his work is not assessable.

The student needs significant instruction.

Student shows some reasoning about rectangles, but answers neither question completely and correctly.

Student B

Student B correctly answers "no" to question 1, but his response is incomplete in that he is unclear as to why the given measures will not make a rectangle. In question 2, he gives factor pairs of 60 as if 60 is the area rather than the perimeter of the tile arrangements.

The student needs some instruction.

Student answers only one of the two questions completely and correctly *OR* student answers both questions, but the justification in question 1 is incomplete *AND* the list in question 2 is not exhaustive.

Student C

Student C correctly explains that the given framing material would not form a rectangle. Her justification with words and diagrams implies the property of rectangles that opposite sides must be equal. However, in question 2, she lists factor pairs of 60.

The student's work needs to be revised.

Student answers questions 1 and 2 correctly, but gives an incomplete explanation in question 1, *OR* student answers question 1 completely but fails to provide an exhaustive list in question 2.

Student D

Student D answers question 1 correctly. His justification does not explain why "the 10s have to have a 20 between them," but his drawing suggests why this is needed. Student D gives three correct rectangles in question 2 and even correctly finds their areas, but his list is not thorough.

Student E

Student E's explanation in question 1 is complete in that she explicitly states "opposite sides have to be equal" and shows how the given perimeter would not form a closed shape. In question 2, Student E explains her system for generating possible perimeters, but she fails to provide a complete list.

The student's work meets the essential demands of the task.

Student answers both questions completely and correctly.

Student F

Student F provides a sufficient explanation for his response to question 1; his list of possible rectangles of perimeter 60 is correct and exhaustive.

Framing Materials

This problem gives you the chance to

- *apply properties of rectangles*
- *explain your reasoning*
- *find dimensions of rectangles*

1. Suppose a 60-inch strip of framing material was bent into segments of 10 inches, 10 inches, 20 inches, and 20 inches, in that order. Can this strip of metal, bent at these marks, form a rectangular frame? Explain why or why not.

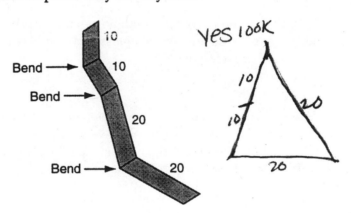

Yes look

2. You are given several 60-inch strips of framing material. Each strip is to be used to make a frame that encloses 1-inch square tiles. Give the dimensions of all the possible rectangular frames that can be made using the strips.

5,5,5,5, 10,10,10,10

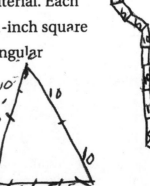

Framing Materials

This problem gives you the chance to

- *apply properties of rectangles*
- *explain your reasoning*
- *find dimensions of rectangles*

1. Suppose a 60-inch strip of framing material was bent into segments of 10 inches, 10 inches, 20 inches, and 20 inches, in that order. Can this strip of metal, bent at these marks, form a rectangular frame? Explain why or why not.

no because it doesn't have the right size of bends-

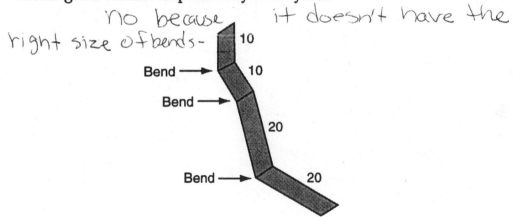

Bend —→ 10

Bend —→ 10

20

Bend —→ 20

2. You are given several 60-inch strips of framing material. Each strip is to be used to make a frame that encloses 1-inch square tiles. Give the dimensions of all the possible rectangular frames that can be made using the strips.

60×1   30×2   15×4   3×20   12×5

6×10

Framing Materials

This problem gives you the chance to
- *apply properties of rectangles*
- *explain your reasoning*
- *find dimensions of rectangles*

1. Suppose a 60-inch strip of framing material was bent into segments of 10 inches, 10 inches, 20 inches, and 20 inches, in that order. Can this strip of metal, bent at these marks, form a rectangular frame? Explain why or why not.

no, Because you have the short strips right beside each other and the long one each other also. It would look like this. They wouldn't touch.

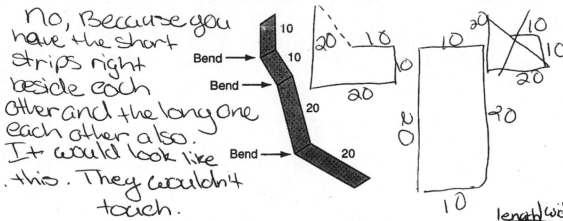

2. You are given several 60-inch strips of framing material. Each strip is to be used to make a frame that encloses 1-inch square tiles. Give the dimensions of all the possible rectangular frames that can be made using the strips.

length	width
1x	60
2x	30
3x	20
4x	15
5x	12
6x	10

Student D

Framing Materials

This problem gives you the chance to

- *apply properties of rectangles*
- *explain your reasoning*
- *find dimensions of rectangles*

1. Suppose a 60-inch strip of framing material was bent into segments of 10 inches, 10 inches, 20 inches, and 20 inches, in that order. Can this strip of metal, bent at these marks, form a rectangular frame? Explain why or why not.

no, Because the ends
won't meet if you
did Bend them.
the 10s have to
have a 20 Between
them.

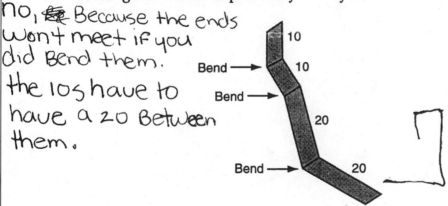

2. You are given several 60-inch strips of framing material. Each strip is to be used to make a frame that encloses 1-inch square tiles. Give the dimensions of all the possible rectangular frames that can be made using the strips.

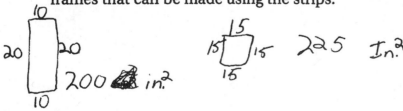

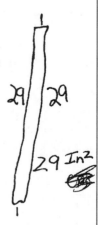

Framing Materials

This problem gives you the chance to
- *apply properties of rectangles*
- *explain your reasoning*
- *find dimensions of rectangles*

1. Suppose a 60-inch strip of framing material was bent into segments of 10 inches, 10 inches, 20 inches, and 20 inches, in that order. Can this strip of metal, bent at these marks, form a rectangular frame? Explain why or why not.

No because it wouldn't be closed. It would look like this.

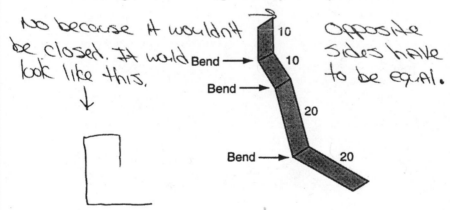

Opposite sides have to be equal.

2. You are given several 60-inch strips of framing material. Each strip is to be used to make a frame that encloses 1-inch square tiles. Give the dimensions of all the possible rectangular frames that can be made using the strips.

All you have to do is Add 2 numbers together And if they equal 30 than you can X's by 2 to get A 60 in. peremeter Around the rectangle

10 + 20 X 2

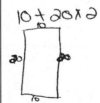

44 16 X 2

5 + 25 X 2

2+28X2

15+15 X 2

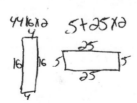

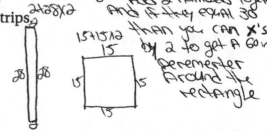

1. Suppose a 60-inch strip of framing material was bent into segments of 10 inches, 10 inches, 20 inches, and 20 inches, in that order. Can this strip of metal, bent at these marks, form a rectangular frame? Explain why or why not.

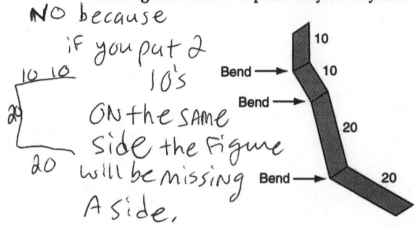

NO because if you put 2 10's ON the same side the Figure will be missing A side.

2. You are given several 60-inch strips of framing material. Each strip is to be used to make a frame that encloses 1-inch square tiles. Give the dimensions of all the possible rectangular frames that can be made using the strips.

more 8×22,
9×21
10×20
11×19
12×18
13×17
14×6

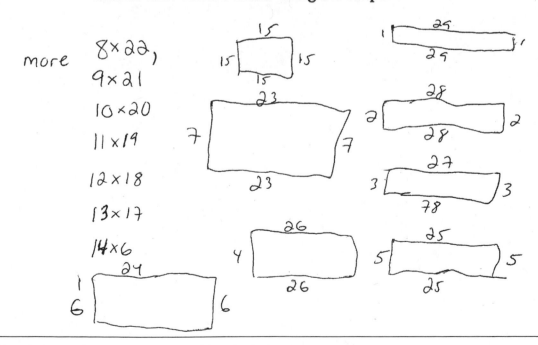

16

Parallel Lines

Use knowledge of corresponding parts.

Determine lengths, angles, and area measures.

Justify reasoning.

Short Task

Task Description

Students are given a grid of three sets of parallel lines. They reason about corresponding parts to determine lengths, angles, and area measures.

Assumed Mathematical Background

It is assumed that students have had experience with angle measurement and properties of shapes and parallel lines.

Core Elements of Performance

- use knowledge of parallel lines and corresponding parts to find congruent lengths, angles, and area
- justify reasoning about geometric relationships

Circumstances

Grouping:	Students complete an individual written response.
Materials:	No special materials are needed for this task.
Estimated time:	15 minutes

Parallel Lines

> **This problem gives you the chance to**
> - *reason about parallel lines, angles, and area*
> - *justify your reasoning*

This grid was made with three sets of parallel lines. The parallel lines in each set are spaced evenly apart.

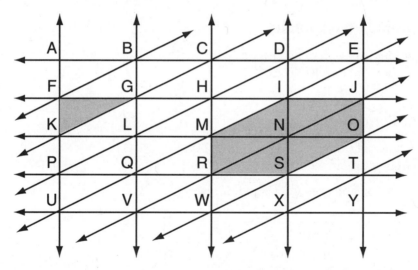

1. Without using a measuring tool, tell which sides of the shaded hexagon (IJOSRM) are the same length as FG. Explain how you know.

© The Regents of the University of California

2. Use letters to name an angle on the grid that is the same size as angle IJO in the hexagon.

3. If the small triangle (FGK) has an area of 10 square units, what is the area of the shaded hexagon? Explain your reasoning.

4. Use letters to name *three* angles on the grid whose sum is 180 degrees. Explain how you knew the sum of these angles is 180 degrees.

© The Regents of the University of California

Task **A Sample Solution**

1. Segments IJ and RS are the same length as segment FG. Segment FG is the long leg of a right triangle and corresponds to all the other long legs of right triangles on the grid, since the parallel lines are evenly spaced. IJ and RS are the only sides of the hexagon that are also long legs of right triangles.

2. Angle ABG or angle GFK or any other right angle is the same size as angle IJO.

3. 60 square units. The hexagon is made up of 6 congruent triangles—IJN, ONJ, ONS, SRN, MNR, MNI—and each is congruent to triangle FGK. Since triangle FGK is 10 square units, the hexagon is 6 × 10 = 60 square units.

4. Solution A: The three angles of any triangle have a sum of 180°. So together, the angles KFG, FGK, and GKF have a sum of 180°.

   Solution B: A straight line forms a 180° angle. So any three angles that together form a straight line sum to 180°. Angles MNI, INJ, and JNO have a sum of 180°.

   Solution C: Interior angles on the same side of the transversal (a line intersecting parallel lines) sum to 180°. For example, two parallel lines are UE and VJ, a transversal is the line CW, and two interior angles on the same side of CW are angles IMR and MRN. Angles IMN and NMR together make the first interior angle IMR. Therefore, angles IMN, NMR, and MRN have a sum of 180°.

Using this Task

For Formal Assessment

After handing out the task to the students, review the aims of the assessment in the box at the top of the activity page. Because this task is short and straightforward, it would be appropriate to simply hand out the task and leave students to individually read and answer the questions.

Issues for Classroom Use

This task does not require formal geometric responses, such as reference to geometric properties. It is expected that middle school students will use visual reasoning and basic knowledge of angles, triangles, and parallel lines to answer the questions.

Characterizing Performance

Task 16

This section offers a characterization of student responses and provides indications of the ways in which the students were successful or unsuccessful in engaging with and completing the task. The descriptions are keyed to the *Core Elements of Performance*. Our global descriptions of student work range from "The student needs significant instruction" to "The student's work meets the essential demands of the task." Samples of student work that exemplify these descriptions of performance are included below, accompanied by commentary on central aspects of each student's response. These sample responses are *representative;* they may not mirror the global description of performance in all respects, being weaker in some and stronger in others.

The characterization of student responses for this task is based on these *Core Elements of Performance:*

1. Use knowledge of parallel lines and corresponding parts to find congruent lengths, angles, and area.
2. Justify reasoning about geometric relationships.

Descriptions of Student Work

The student needs significant instruction.

Student may answer some identification questions correctly, but offers no justification.

Student A

Student A gives a correct line segment in question 1, but his statement cannot qualify as justification. He names a correct angle in question 2 though with incorrect notation. The answer to question 3 is incorrect and there is no explanation. In question 4, Student A gives an incorrect response naming three right angles, rather than three angles whose sum is 180°, and again offers no explanation.

The student needs some instruction.

Student answers several identification questions correctly and offers some justification, but justification is weak or unreasonable.

Student B

Student B answers questions 1, 2, and 3 correctly. The justification she provides in question 1 is weak but in question 3 is sufficient. In question 4, Student B names three line segments, not angles. Her justification shows confusion about lines and angle measures.

The student's work needs to be revised.

Student answers all questions correctly but some justifications are missing, incomplete or not clearly expressed.

Student C

Student C answers all four questions correctly, but offers justification for question 3 only.

Student D

Student D answers questions 1–3 correctly. For question 4 her notation is imprecise in that angle R (for example) could be any one of several angles. Her justification for question 1 is weak. One must read into her justification that she is using the given information that the lines are evenly spaced apart and parallel.

The student's work meets the essential demands of the task.

Student answers all questions correctly and provides reasonable and clearly expressed justifications.

Student E

Student E answers all questions correctly and provides clear and complete justifications in questions 3 and 4. The student uses a visual justification in response to question 1. It would have been stronger had he explicitly stated that since the parallel lines are evenly spaced, then segments IJ and RS are each the same length as segment FG.

Student A

1. Without using a measuring tool, tell which sides of the shaded hexagon (IJOSRM) are the same length as FG. Explain how you know. I J because it is the exact Same Shape

2. Use letters to name an angle on the grid that is the same size as angle IJO in the hexagon. B ,C, H

3. If the small triangle (FGK) has an area of 10 square units, what is the area of the shaded hexagon? Explain your reasoning. 4⁸ Square units

4. Use letters to name *three* angles on the grid whose sum is 180 degrees. Explain how you knew the sum of these angles is 180 degrees. L ,Q ,R   S, x ,Y   R,W,X

1. Without using a measuring tool, tell which sides of the shaded hexagon (IJOSRM) are the same length as FG. Explain how you know. IJ + SR because they look like they are exactly like FG.

2. Use letters to name an angle on the grid that is the same size as angle IJO in the hexagon. CDI angle

3. If the small triangle (FGK) has an area of 10 square units, what is the area of the shaded hexagon? Explain your reasoning. 60 square units because its 6 of the same triangles as FGK so you times 6 by 10.

4. Use letters to name *three* angles on the grid whose sum is 180 degrees. Explain how you knew the sum of these angles is 180 degrees. AB, CD & GH. because I know 180° is a straight line + they were straight lines.

1. Without using a measuring tool, tell which sides of the shaded hexagon (IJOSRM) are the same length as FG. Explain how you know.

   I to J and R to S

2. Use letters to name an angle on the grid that is the same size as angle IJO in the hexagon.

   MRS

3. If the small triangle (FGK) has an area of 10 square units, what is the area of the shaded hexagon? Explain your reasoning.

   60, because the triangle goes into the hexagon 6 times and I times that by 10.

4. Use letters to name *three* angles on the grid whose sum is 180 degrees. Explain how you knew the sum of these angles is 180 degrees.

   JIN + INJ + NJI = 180°

Student D

1. Without using a measuring tool, tell which sides of the shaded hexagon (IJOSRM) are the same length as FG. Explain how you know.

   I S
   R S

   because the are All the lines going straight across, Left to right, and FG is Left to right

2. Use letters to name an angle on the grid that is the same size as angle IJO in the hexagon.

   ∠RMN

3. If the small triangle (FGK) has an area of 10 square units, what is the area of the shaded hexagon? Explain your reasoning.

   60 Square units because there is 10 sq. un. in the (FGK) one and 6 FGk's CAN fit in the Hexagon and 10×6 = 60

4. Use letters to name *three* angles on the grid whose sum is 180 degrees. Explain how you knew the sum of these angles is 180 degrees.

   ∠R+∠S+∠n ∠m+∠N+∠I ∠J+∠O+∠N
   because they Are triangle and All ANGLES ON A triangle Add up to 180°

1. Without using a measuring tool, tell which sides of the shaded hexagon (IJOSRM) are the same length as FG. Explain how you know.

The lenths IJ and RS are the Same as the length FG
Same length

2. Use letters to name an angle on the grid that is the same size as angle IJO in the hexagon. Angles KFG, BCH, QRW, RSX, are all the same as angle IJO on the Hexagon They're all right angles

3. If the small triangle (FGK) has an area of 10 square units, what is the area of the shaded hexagon? Explain your reasoning. It would be 60 sq units because there is 6 of those triangles congruent to FGK

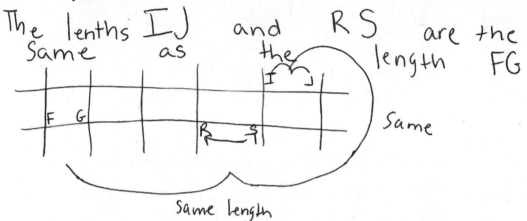

4. Use letters to name *three* angles on the grid whose sum is 180 degrees. Explain how you knew the sum of these angles is 180 degrees. < PQL + MQL + RQM = because it equals a striaght line
180°

Tangram

Task Description

Students are given a Tangram, an oriental puzzle made up of geometric shapes. They determine what fractional part each piece represents and give explanations to justify their names.

Assumed Mathematical Background

It is assumed that students have a background in rational numbers.

Core Elements of Performance

■ correctly identify fractional parts of a whole using spatial and analytical reasoning

■ justify fractional names

Circumstances

Grouping:	Students complete an individual written response.
Materials:	scissors
Estimated time:	10 minutes

Tangram

> **This problem gives you the chance to**
> - *identify fractional parts*
> - *justify fractional names*

Below is an oriental puzzle called a Tangram. It is made up of geometric shapes. For this task, consider the area of the whole puzzle, the large square, to be 1 whole unit.

If the area of the original square is 1 whole unit, what fractional part of the whole does each tangram shape represent? (You may cut out the Tangram puzzle found on page 239 to help you with this task.)

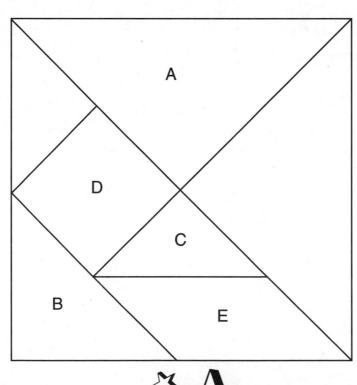

© *The Regents of the University of California*

1. Write the fractional part of each shape in relation to the whole and describe how you figured it out.

Shape	Fraction and your explanation
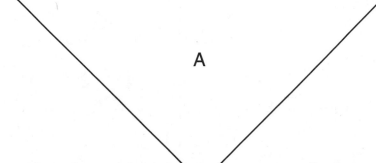 A	
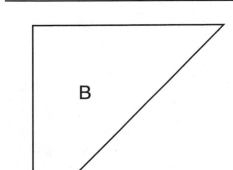 B	
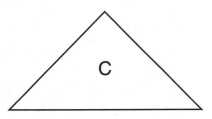 C	

© The Regents of the University of California

Shape	Fraction and your explanation
D	
E	

© *The Regents of the University of California*

Name _____ Date _____

Tangram Puzzle Cutout

© The Regents of the University of California

Task **A Sample Solution**

Solution A

$A = \frac{1}{4}$: Four of these triangles would make the entire square, so piece A is $\frac{1}{4}$ of the square.

$B = \frac{1}{8}$: Piece A can be made by putting 2 B-pieces together. So, B is equal to $\frac{1}{2}$ of A or $\frac{1}{8}$ of the whole square.

$C = \frac{1}{16}$: Piece B can be made by putting 2 C-pieces together. So, C is equal to $\frac{1}{2}$ of B or $\frac{1}{16}$ of the whole square.

$D = \frac{1}{8}$: Piece D can be made by putting 2 C-pieces together. D is twice C or $\frac{2}{16}$ which equals $\frac{1}{8}$ of the whole square.

$E = \frac{1}{8}$: Piece E can also be made by putting 2 C-pieces together. So, E is also $\frac{1}{8}$ of the whole square.

Solution B

C is the smallest piece and can be used a whole number of times to make each other piece. You can cut out piece C, determine the number of C-sized pieces that are needed to make the whole square and then determine the relationship of C to each other piece. Since it takes 16 C-pieces to exactly cover the whole square, $C = \frac{1}{16}$.

$A = \frac{1}{4}$: 4 Cs make up A. Therefore $A = \frac{4}{16} = \frac{1}{4}$ of the whole square.

$B = \frac{1}{8}$: 2 Cs make up B. Therefore $B = \frac{2}{16} = \frac{1}{8}$ of the whole square.

$C = \frac{1}{16}$: 16 Cs make up the whole square.

$D = \frac{1}{8}$: 2 Cs make up D. Therefore $D = \frac{2}{16} = \frac{1}{8}$ of the whole square.

$E = \frac{1}{8}$: 2 Cs make up E. Therefore $E = \frac{2}{16} = \frac{1}{8}$ of the whole square.

Using this Task

For Formal Assessment

Review the aims of the assessment in the box at the top of the first activity page. Read the problem aloud to your students. Because this task is short and straightforward, it would be appropriate to simply hand out the task and leave students to individually read and answer the questions.

Issues for Classroom Use

Students may approach this task using different forms of reasoning. Some prefer a visual approach while others prefer an analytical one. Some combination of both is usually necessary for yielding accurate responses.

You may wish to extend this task by using some of the ideas that follow.

- Make a design from the tangram pieces that has an area $\frac{1}{2}$ of the original puzzle. Sketch your design. Explain how you know your design has an area $\frac{1}{2}$ of the original puzzle.

- Make a design from the tangram pieces that has an area $\frac{3}{4}$ of the original puzzle. Sketch your design. Explain how you know your design has an area $\frac{3}{4}$ of the original puzzle.

- Make some designs of your own using different pieces from the tangram puzzle. For each of your designs, find its area compared to the original puzzle having an area of 1 square unit.

Task

Characterizing Performance

This section offers a characterization of student responses and provides indications of the ways in which the students were successful or unsuccessful in engaging with and completing the task. The descriptions are keyed to the *Core Elements of Performance*. Our global descriptions of student work range from "The student needs significant instruction" to "The student's work meets the essential demands of the task." Samples of student work that exemplify these descriptions of performance are included below, accompanied by commentary on central aspects of each student's response. These sample responses are *representative;* they may not mirror the global description of performance in all respects, being weaker in some and stronger in others.

The characterization of student responses for this task is based on these *Core Elements of Performance:*

1. Correctly identify fractional parts of a whole using spatial and analytical reasoning.
2. Justify fractional names.

Descriptions of Student Work

The student's work cannot be assessed.

Student A

Student A does not relate the tangram pieces to the whole square. It is not clear how he determines his measures. Student A's work does not reveal any understanding of fractions and therefore cannot be assessed.

The student needs significant instruction.

Student demonstrates some reasoning about fractions and may or may not identify some fractional parts correctly, but offers insufficient justification for names.

Student B

Student B uses fractions to name pieces but does not name a single tangram piece correctly and his justifications show a serious lack of understanding about fractions.

The student needs some instruction.

Student identifies some fractional parts correctly and provides some justification for those names, although justification is weak.

Student C

Student C names two pieces correctly (A and B) and makes attempts at justifying these names, but her justification is quite weak. For example, Student C states "8 pieces in the whole 1 pieces filled in" but, neither states nor shows in her diagram that 8 B-pieces make up the whole square.

The student's work needs to be revised.

Student identifies most fractional parts correctly and offers complete justification for most names, although some parts are labeled incorrectly *OR* some justification is incomplete.

Student D

Student D labels three tangram pieces correctly (A, B, and C) and provides justification in the form of diagrams, showing how, for example with C, 16 C-pieces fit into the whole square. For pieces D and E, she shows that each is equivalent to two Cs, but she errs in implying that $\frac{2}{16} = \frac{1}{32}$.

Student E

Student E gives correct names for all tangram pieces. She makes attempts at justification, but her explanations are weak. For example, in her "explanations" for pieces B and C, she does not make clear which pieces she is dividing in half. With pieces D and E, she does not fully explain how she relates them to piece C.

The student's work meets the essential demands of the task.

Student identifies all fractional parts correctly and provides complete justification for all names.

Student F

Student F correctly identifies all fractional parts and provides sufficient justification. In justifying both pieces A and C, he relates each piece to the whole square. He also justifies pieces B, D, and E by relating each of them to piece C.

Student A

1. Write the fractional part of each shape in relation to the whole and describe how you figured it out.

Shape	Fraction and your explanation
A (triangle)	24 ½ — Because A is a triangle it has 24½ of area, because each slant counts as half.
B (triangle)	12 — Because B is slanted on a right. angle and is half the value of a Parallelogram
C (triangle)	13½ — Because each square count is 1 square unit and letter c is on an angle.

Shape	Fraction and your explanation
D	15 Because 15 has 2 left angles and is slanted on a right angles.
E	18 Because E is a parallelogram and has 4 angles slanted.

1. Write the fractional part of each shape in relation to the whole and describe how you figured it out.

Shape	Fraction and your explanation
A	1/2 because It take's almost all of the whole
B	1/4 bigger then most of the pieces
C	1/3 because bigger but smaller then the bigger ones.

Shape	Fraction and your explanation
D	1/3 It's the same as the other 1/3 but littler.
E	1/4 It's the same as the other 1/4 but smaller.

Student C

1. Write the fractional part of each shape in relation to the whole and describe how you figured it out.

Shape	Fraction and your explanation
A	I think that the (A) would be 1/4 of the whole 1 whole .25 like money
B	$\frac{1}{8}$ 8 pieces in the whole 1 pieces Filled in.
C	

Student C

Shape	Fraction and your explanation
D	
E	If I related this to cents is would be only .20¢ because it is not all Fill in like .25¢ would be.

1. Write the fractional part of each shape in relation to the whole and describe how you figured it out.

Shape	Fraction and your explanation
A	1/4
B	1/8
C	1/16

Shape	Fraction and your explanation
D	$\frac{1}{32}$
E	$\frac{1}{32}$

1. Write the fractional part of each shape in relation to the whole and describe how you figured it out.

Shape	Fraction and your explanation
A	$\frac{1}{4}$
B	$\frac{1}{8}$ $\frac{1}{4}$ divid en half you have $\frac{1}{8}$
C	$\frac{1}{16}$ -18 together

Shape	Fraction and your explanation
D	$\frac{1}{8}$ because put 2c and you get $\frac{1}{8}$
E	$\frac{1}{8}$ because you can fit two C. in one

1. Write the fractional part of each shape in relation to the whole and describe how you figured it out.

Shape	Fraction and your explanation
A	$\frac{4}{16} = \frac{1}{4}$ Because 4 A's could make 1 sq. unit.
B	$\frac{2}{16} = \frac{1}{8}$ because if you take All the shapes and divide them All up to look like C you get 16 C's and B is divided into
C	$\frac{1}{16}$ Because if you divide All the shapes to look like C you get 16 and so C is $\frac{1}{16}$.

254

Student F

Shape	Fraction and your explanation
D	$\frac{2}{16} = \frac{1}{8}$ Because if you divide All the slopes up to look like C there is 16 C's and 2 C's fit in d. and $\frac{2}{16}$ is equal to $\frac{1}{8}$.
E	$\frac{2}{16} = \frac{1}{8}$ Because if you divide All the shapes up to look like C you get 16 C's and 2 C's fit in E. and $\frac{2}{16}$ is equal to $\frac{1}{8}$.

Tile Signs

Short Task

Task Description

Students are asked to find the dimensions of all rectangles that can be made from 80 square tiles. They are then asked to find the perimeter and area of these rectangles. Then students explain which rectangles they think would not be good for making word signs using two different colors of tiles.

Assumed Mathematical Background

It is assumed that students have had experience with finding the area and perimeter of rectangles.

Core Elements of Performance

- use knowledge of factor pairs to determine dimensions of rectangles

- find area and perimeter for each rectangle described

- reason about dimensions of rectangles for making tile signs and justify choices

Circumstances

Grouping:	Students complete an individual written response.
Materials:	No special materials are needed for this task.
Estimated time:	15 minutes

Tile Signs

This problem gives you the chance to

- *find dimensions, perimeter, and area measures of rectangles*
- *reason about size*

You can use two different colors of tiles to make words appear in rectangular arrangements, like the one shown here.

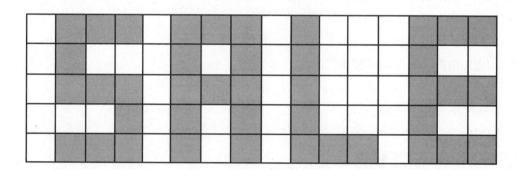

1. The above arrangement contains 80 tiles. What are the dimensions of all the different rectangles that can be made with 80 tiles?

2. Which of the rectangles that you listed in question 1 would NOT make good choices for making words using two different color tiles? Explain why.

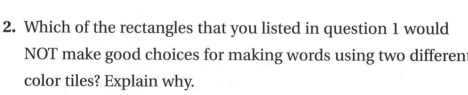

© The Regents of the University of California

3. Each tile is 1 inch long on each side. What is the area of each rectangle that you described in question 1?

4. A flat, metal strip can be used to wrap around and frame each rectangular tile sign. The strip helps to hold the tiles in place. How many inches of framing material would you need to go around the edge of each of the rectangles you described in question 1?

© The Regents of the University of California

Task **A Sample Solution**

18

1. The dimensions of all the rectangles that can be made are
   - 1 tile by 80 tiles
   - 2 tiles by 40 tiles
   - 4 tiles by 20 tiles
   - 5 tiles by 16 tiles
   - 8 tiles by 10 tiles

2. Both a 1-by-80 and a 2-by-40 rectangle would not be good choices for making signs with two colors. Depending on how you orient them, either their height or width would not provide enough space for making letters. A 4-by-20 rectangle is also not that good a choice since many letters cannot be made with a height of only 4. An 8-by-10 rectangle is also a limited choice, since it is not very wide. But it depends on what you want the sign to say. An 8-by-10 rectangle is almost a square shape, so if you don't want to make two rows of letters, you could write a short word. However, it would be perfect for the word *HI*.

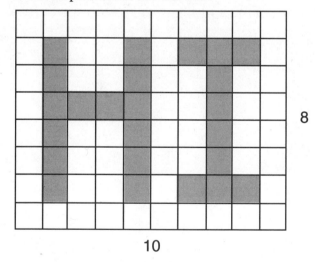

3. The area of each rectangle is 80 square inches.

4. The flat strip that frames each rectangle represents the perimeter. The perimeter of each rectangle in inches is
   - 1-by-80: 162 inches (80 + 80 + 1 + 1 = 162)
   - 2-by-40: 84 inches (40 + 40 + 2 + 2 = 84)
   - 4-by-20: 48 inches (20 + 20 + 4 + 4 = 48)
   - 5-by-16: 42 inches (16 + 16 + 5 + 5 = 42)
   - 8-by-10: 36 inches (10 + 10 + 8 + 8 = 36)

Characterizing Performance

This section offers a characterization of student responses and provides indications of the ways in which the students were successful or unsuccessful in engaging with and completing the task. The descriptions are keyed to the *Core Elements of Performance*. Our global descriptions of student work range from "The student needs significant instruction" to "The student's work meets the essential demands of the task." Samples of student work that exemplify these descriptions of performance are included below, accompanied by commentary on central aspects of each student's response. These sample responses are *representative;* they may not mirror the global description of performance in all respects, being weaker in some and stronger in others.

The characterization of student responses for this task is based on these *Core Elements of Performance:*
1. Use knowledge of factor pairs to determine dimensions of rectangles.
2. Find area and perimeter for each rectangle described.
3. Reason about dimensions of rectangles for making tile signs and justify choices.

Descriptions of Student Work

The student needs significant instruction.

Student may provide some correct answers, but answers two or more questions incompletely, incorrectly, or not at all.

Student A

Student A has some correct answers (two correct rectangles for question 1, provides a partial correct answer for question 2, and has the correct number for the area for question 3) although does not provide a completely correct response for any of the questions.

The student needs some instruction.

Student provides correct answers to most questions, but demonstrates weak understanding of area *OR* perimeter (for example, answers question 3 *OR* question 4 incompletely or incorrectly).

No student examples at this level.

The student's work needs to be revised.

Student provides correct answers to all numerical questions, but one or more pieces are missing (for example, student uses incorrect units of measure, student misses a possible rectangle, and/or student fails to provide justification in question 2).

Student B

Student B provides correct numerical answers to all questions. His response to question 2 is weak, only stating that one kind of rectangle will not work and he gives insufficient justification.

The student's work meets the essential demands of the task.

Student correctly answers all questions and in question 2, student provides adequate support for why at least two of the rectangles would not make good signs.

Student C

Student C correctly answers all questions. The student provides sufficient justification for two kinds of rectangles in response to question 2, along with illustrations. The responses to questions 3 and 4 are very clear and precise and have the correct units.

Tile Signs

This problem gives you the chance to

- *find dimensions, perimeter, and area measures of rectangles*
- *reason about size*

You can use two different colors of tiles to make words appear in rectangular arrangements, like the one shown here.

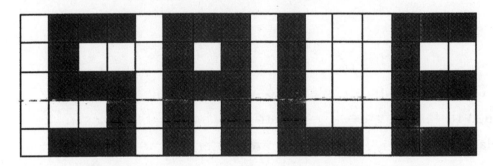

1. The above arrangement contains 80 tiles. What are the dimensions of all the different rectangles that can be made with 80 tiles?

   ① 40 x 40
   ② 16 X 5
   ③ 80 X 1

2. Which of the rectangles that you listed in question 1 would NOT make good choices for making words using two different color tiles? Explain why.

   80x1 would not be good choice 'coz it would be to long and to hard to make.

3. Each tile is 1 inch long on each side. What is the area of each rectangle that you described in question 1?

8 inches cuz that what the dimentions are.

4. A flat, metal strip can be used to wrap around and frame each rectangular tile sign. The strip helps to hold the tiles in place. How many inches of framing material would you need to go around the edge of each of the rectangles you described in question 1?

For #2 on #1 you'll need 20 'cuz thats how much is on the outside.
#1 You'll need 40 'cuz well, it explains up there.
On #3 you'll need 8.

Tile Signs

This problem gives you the chance to

- *find dimensions, perimeter, and area measures of rectangles*
- *reason about size*

You can use two different colors of tiles to make words appear in rectangular arrangements, like the one shown here.

1. The above arrangement contains 80 tiles. What are the dimensions of all the different rectangles that can be made with 80 tiles?

   1X80 2X40 16X5 10X8 4X20

2. Which of the rectangles that you listed in question 1 would NOT make good choices for making words using two different color tiles? Explain why.

   The one by 80 Because you can't spell any words.

3. Each tile is 1 inch long on each side. What is the area of each rectangle that you described in question 1? 80 sq. Inches.

4. A flat, metal strip can be used to wrap around and frame each rectangular tile sign. The strip helps to hold the tiles in place. How many inches of framing material would you need to go around the edge of each of the rectangles you described in question 1?

1×80 = 162 sq. Inches.

2×40 = 84. sq. Inches.

4×20 = 48. sq. Inches.

5×16 = 42. sq. Inches.

8×10 = 36. sq. Inches.

∞

Tile Signs

This problem gives you the chance to

- *find dimensions, perimeter, and area measures of rectangles*
- *reason about size*

You can use two different colors of tiles to make words appear in rectangular arrangements, like the one shown here.

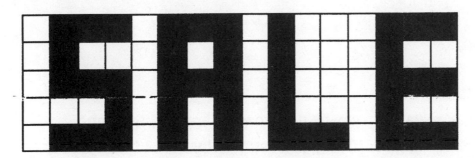

1. The above arrangement contains 80 tiles. What are the dimensions of all the different rectangles that can be made with 80 tiles? *You can make a:*

    1 X 80 - 80 X 1
    2 X 40 - 40 X 2
    4 X 20 - 20 X 4
    5 X 16 - 16 X 5
    8 X 10 - 10 X 8

2. Which of the rectangles that you listed in question 1 would *Good one* NOT make good choices for making words using two different color tiles? Explain why.

1 X 80 and 2 X 40 because the aren't wide enough to to make any letters.

because you can write on this

Bad ones →

3. Each tile is 1 inch long on each side. What is the area of each rectangle that you described in question 1?

1 X 80 — Area : 80
2X 40 — area: 80
4X 20 — area: 80
5X 16 — area: 80
8X 10 — area: 80
80X 1 — area: 80
40X 2 — area: 80
20X 4 — area: 80
16X 5 — area: 80
10X 8 — area: 80

All are 80 sq inches

4. A flat, metal strip can be used to wrap around and frame each rectangular tile sign. The strip helps to hold the tiles in place. How many inches of framing material would you need to go around the edge of each of the rectangles you described in question 1?

1 X 80 → 162 inches ⟵ 80 X 1

2 X 40 → 84 inches ⟵ 40 X 2

4 X 20 → 48 inches ⟵ 20 X 4

5 X 16 → 42 inches ⟵ 16 X 5

8 X 10 → 36 inches ⟵ 10 X 8

This glossary defines a number of the terms that are used to describe the *Dimensions of Balance* table that appears in the package *Introduction*.

Applied power: a task goal—to provide students an opportunity to demonstrate their power over a real-world practical situation, with that as the main criterion for success. This includes choosing mathematical tools appropriately for the problem situation, using them effectively, and interpreting and evaluating the results in relation to the practical needs of the situation. [cf. *illustrative application*]

Checking and evaluating: a mathematical process that involves evaluating the quality of a problem solution in relation to the problem situation (for example, checking calculations; comparing model predictions with data; considering whether a solution is reasonable and appropriate; asking further questions).

Definition of concepts: a task type—such tasks require the clarification of a concept and the generation of a mathematical definition to fit a set of conditions.

Design: a task type that calls for the design, and perhaps construction, of an object (for example, a model building, a scale drawing, a game) together with instructions on how to use the object. The task may include evaluating the results in light of various constraints and desirable features. [cf. *plan*]

Evaluation and recommendation: a task type that calls for collecting and analyzing information bearing on a decision. Students review evidence and make a recommendation based on the evidence. The product is a "consultant" report for a "client."

Exercise: a task type that requires only the application of a learned procedure or a "tool kit" of techniques (for example, adding decimals; solving an equation); the product is simply an answer that is judged for accuracy.

Illustrative application of mathematics: a task goal—to provide the student an opportunity to demonstrate effective use of mathematics in a context outside mathematics. The focus is on the specific piece of mathematics, while the reality and utility of the context as a model of a practical situation are secondary. [cf. *applied power*]

Inferring and drawing conclusions: a mathematical process that involves applying derived results to the original problem situation and interpreting the results in that light.

Modeling and formulating: a mathematical process that involves taking the situation as presented in the task and formulating mathematical statements of the problem to be solved. Working the task involves selecting appropriate representations and relationships to model the problem situation.

Nonroutine problem: a task type that presents an unfamiliar problem situation, one that students are not expected to have analyzed before or have not met regularly in the curriculum. Such problems demand some flexibility of thinking, and adaptation or extension of previous knowledge. They may be situated in a context that students have not encountered in the curriculum; they may involve them in the introduction of concepts and techniques that will be explicitly taught at a later stage; they may involve the discovery of connections among mathematical ideas.

Open-ended: a task structure that requires some questions to be posed by the student. Therefore open-ended tasks often have multiple solutions and may allow for a variety of problem-solving strategies. They provide students with a wide range of possibilities for choosing and making decisions. [cf. *open-middle*]

Open investigation: an open-ended task type that invites exploration of a problem situation with the aim of discovering and establishing facts and relationships. The criteria for evaluating student performance are based on exploring thoroughly, generalizing, justifying, and explaining with clarity and economy.

Open-middle: a task structure in which the question and its answer are well-defined (there is a clear recognizable "answer") but with a variety of strategies or methods for approaching the problem. [cf. *open-ended*]

Plan: a task type that calls for the design of a sequence of activities, or a schedule of events, where time is an essential variable and where the need to organize the efforts of others is implied. [cf. *design*]

Pure mathematics: a task type—one that provides the student an opportunity to demonstrate power over a situation within a mathematics "microworld." This may be an open investigation, a nonroutine problem, or a technical exercise.

Reporting: a mathematical process that involves communicating to a specified "audience" what has been learned about the problem. Components of a successful response include explaining why the results follow from the problem formulation, explaining manipulations of the formalism, and drawing conclusions from the information presented, with some evaluation.

Re-presentation of information: a task type that requires interpretation of information presented in one form and its translation to some different form (for example, write a set of verbal directions that would allow a listener to reproduce a given geometric design; represent the information in a piece of text with a graphic or a symbolic expression).

Review and critique: a task type that involves reflection on curriculum materials (for example, one might review a piece of student work, identify errors, and make suggestions for revision; pose further questions; produce notes on a recently learned topic).

Scaffolding: the degree of detailed step-by-step guidance that a task prompt provides a student.

Task length: the time that should be allowed for students to work on the task. Also important is the length of time students are asked by the task to think independently—the reasoning length. (For a single well-defined question, reasoning length will equal the task length; for a task consisting of many parts, the reasoning length can be much shorter—essentially the time for the longest part.)

Transforming and manipulating: a mathematical process that involves manipulating the mathematical forms in which the problem is expressed, usually with the aim of transforming them into other equivalent forms that represent "solutions" to the problem (for example, dividing one fraction by another, making a geometric construction, solving equations, plotting graphs, finding the derivative of a function).